NIST Special Publication 800-137

Information Security Continuous Monitoring (ISCM) for Federal Information Systems and Organizations

NIST

National Institute of Standards and Technology

U.S. Department of Commerce

Kelley Dempsey
Nirali Shah Chawla
Arnold Johnson
Ronald Johnston
Alicia Clay Jones
Angela Orebaugh
Matthew Scholl
Kevin Stine

INFORMATION SECURITY

Computer Security Division
Information Technology Laboratory
National Institute of Standards and Technology
Gaithersburg, MD 20899-8930

SEPTEMBER 2011

U.S. Department of Commerce
Rebecca M. Blank, Acting Secretary

National Institute of Standards and Technology
Patrick D. Gallagher, Under Secretary for Standards and Technology and Director

Reports on Computer Systems Technology

The Information Technology Laboratory (ITL) at the National Institute of Standards and Technology (NIST) promotes the U.S. economy and public welfare by providing technical leadership for the nation's measurement and standards infrastructure. ITL develops tests, test methods, reference data, proof of concept implementations, and technical analyses to advance the development and productive use of information technology. ITL's responsibilities include the development of management, administrative, technical, and physical standards and guidelines for the cost-effective security and privacy of other than national security-related information in federal information systems. The Special Publication 800-series reports on ITL's research, guidelines, and outreach efforts in information system security, and its collaborative activities with industry, government, and academic organizations.

Authority

This publication has been developed by NIST to further its statutory responsibilities under the Federal Information Security Management Act (FISMA), Public Law (P.L.) 107-347. NIST is responsible for developing information security standards and guidelines, including minimum requirements for federal information systems, but such standards and guidelines shall not apply to national security systems without the express approval of appropriate federal officials exercising policy authority over such systems. This guideline is consistent with the requirements of the Office of Management and Budget (OMB) Circular A-130, Section 8b(3), Securing Agency Information Systems, as analyzed in Circular A-130, Appendix IV: Analysis of Key Sections. Supplemental information is provided in Circular A-130, Appendix III.

Nothing in this publication should be taken to contradict the standards and guidelines made mandatory and binding on federal agencies by the Secretary of Commerce under statutory authority. Nor should these guidelines be interpreted as altering or superseding the existing authorities of the Secretary of Commerce, Director of the OMB, or any other federal official. This publication may be used by nongovernmental organizations on a voluntary basis and is not subject to copyright in the United States. Attribution would, however, be appreciated by NIST.

NIST Special Publication 800-137, 80 pages

(September 2011)

National Institute of Standards and Technology
Attn: Computer Security Division, Information Technology Laboratory
100 Bureau Drive (Mail Stop 8930) Gaithersburg, MD 20899-8930
Electronic mail: 800-137comments@nist.gov

Acknowledgements

The authors, Kelley Dempsey, Arnold Johnson, Matthew Scholl and Kevin Stine of the National Institute of Standards and Technology (NIST), Ronald Johnston of the Department of Defense Chief Information Officer, Defense-wide Information Assurance Program (DOD-CIO, DIAP), Alicia Clay Jones and Angela Orebaugh of Booz Allen Hamilton, and Nirali Shah Chawla of PricewaterhouseCoopers LLP (PwC), wish to thank their colleagues who reviewed drafts of this document and contributed to its technical content. The authors would like to acknowledge their colleagues for their keen and insightful assistance with technical issues throughout the development of the document. And finally, the authors gratefully acknowledge and appreciate the significant contributions from individuals and organizations in the public and private sectors whose thoughtful and constructive comments improved the overall quality and usefulness of this publication.

Table of Contents

CHAPTER ONE INTRODUCTION 1

    1.1   BACKGROUND 2
    1.2   RELATIONSHIP TO OTHER PUBLICATIONS..2
    1.3   PURPOSE..3
    1.4   TARGET AUDIENCE..3
    1.5   ORGANIZATION OF THIS SPECIAL PUBLICATION 4

CHAPTER TWO THE FUNDAMENTALS 5

    2.1   ORGANIZATION-WIDE VIEW OF ISCM..6
    2.2   ONGOING SYSTEM AUTHORIZATIONS 10
    2.3   ROLE OF AUTOMATION IN ISCM..12
    2.4   ISCM ROLES AND RESPONSIBILITIES 13

CHAPTER THREE THE PROCESS 16

    3.1   DEFINE ISCM STRATEGY...17
    3.2   ESTABLISH AN ISCM PROGRAM..24
    3.3   IMPLEMENT AN ISCM PROGRAM 30
    3.4   ANALYZE DATA AND REPORT FINDINGS 31
    3.5   RESPOND TO FINDINGS 33
    3.6   REVIEW AND UPDATE THE MONITORING PROGRAM AND STRATEGY 34

APPENDIX A REFERENCES A-1

APPENDIX B GLOSSARY...B-1

APPENDIX C ACRONYMS C-1

APPENDIX D TECHNOLOGIES FOR ENABLING ISCM D-1

EXECUTIVE SUMMARY

In today's environment where many, if not all, of an organization's mission-critical functions are dependent upon information technology, the ability to manage this technology and to assure confidentiality, integrity, and availability of information is now also mission-critical. In designing the enterprise architecture and corresponding security architecture, an organization seeks to securely meet the IT infrastructure needs of its governance structure, missions, and core business processes. Information security is a dynamic process that must be effectively and proactively managed for an organization to identify and respond to new vulnerabilities, evolving threats, and an organization's constantly changing enterprise architecture and operational environment.

The Risk Management Framework (RMF) developed by NIST,[1] describes a disciplined and structured process that integrates information security and risk management activities into the system development life cycle. Ongoing monitoring is a critical part of that risk management process. In addition, an organization's overall security architecture and accompanying security program are monitored to ensure that organization-wide operations remain within an acceptable level of risk, despite any changes that occur. Timely, relevant, and accurate information is vital, particularly when resources are limited and agencies must prioritize their efforts.

> Information security continuous monitoring (ISCM) is defined as maintaining ongoing awareness of information security, vulnerabilities, and threats to support organizational risk management decisions.

Any effort or process intended to support ongoing monitoring of information security across an organization begins with leadership defining a comprehensive ISCM strategy encompassing technology, processes, procedures, operating environments, and people. This strategy:

- Is grounded in a clear understanding of organizational risk tolerance and helps officials set priorities and manage risk consistently throughout the organization;

- Includes metrics that provide meaningful indications of security status at all organizational tiers;

- Ensures continued effectiveness of all security controls;

- Verifies compliance with information security requirements derived from organizational missions/business functions, federal legislation, directives, regulations, policies, and standards/guidelines;

- Is informed by all organizational IT assets and helps to maintain visibility into the security of the assets;

- Ensures knowledge and control of changes to organizational systems and environments of operation; and

- Maintains awareness of threats and vulnerabilities.

---

[1] See NIST Special Publication (SP) 800-37, as amended, *Guide for Applying the Risk Management Framework to Federal Information Systems A Security Life Cycle Approach.*

An ISCM program is established to collect information in accordance with preestablished metrics, utilizing information readily available in part through implemented security controls. Organizational officials collect and analyze the data regularly and as often as needed to manage risk as appropriate for each organizational tier. This process involves the entire organization, from senior leaders providing governance and strategic vision to individuals developing, implementing, and operating individual systems in support of the organization's core missions and business processes. Subsequently, determinations are made from an organizational perspective on whether to conduct mitigation activities or to reject, transfer, or accept risk.

Organizations' security architectures, operational security capabilities, and monitoring processes will improve and mature over time to better respond to the dynamic threat and vulnerability landscape. An organization's ISCM strategy and program are routinely reviewed for relevance and are revised as needed to increase visibility into assets and awareness of vulnerabilities. This further enables data-driven control of the security of an organization's information infrastructure, and increase organizational resilience.

Organization-wide monitoring cannot be efficiently achieved through manual processes alone or through automated processes alone. Where manual processes are used, the processes are repeatable and verifiable to enable consistent implementation. Automated processes, including the use of automated support tools (e.g., vulnerability scanning tools, network scanning devices), can make the process of continuous monitoring more cost-effective, consistent, and efficient. Many of the technical security controls defined in NIST Special Publication (SP) 800-53, *Recommended Security Controls for Federal Information Systems and Organizations,* as amended, are good candidates for monitoring using automated tools and techniques. Real-time monitoring of implemented technical controls using automated tools can provide an organization with a much more dynamic view of the effectiveness of those controls and the security posture of the organization. It is important to recognize that with any comprehensive information security program, all implemented security controls, including management and operational controls, must be regularly assessed for effectiveness, even if the monitoring of such controls cannot be automated or is not easily automated.

Organizations take the following steps to establish, implement, and maintain ISCM:

- **Define** an ISCM strategy;

- **Establish** an ISCM program;

- **Implement** an ISCM program;

- **Analyze** data and **Report** findings;

- **Respond** to findings; and

- **Review and Update** the ISCM strategy and program.

A robust ISCM program thus enables organizations to move from compliance-driven risk management to data-driven risk management providing organizations with information necessary to support risk response decisions, security status information, and ongoing insight into security control effectiveness.

CHAPTER ONE

INTRODUCTION

*I*nformation security continuous monitoring (ISCM) is defined as maintaining ongoing awareness of information security, vulnerabilities, and threats to support organizational risk management decisions. [2] This publication specifically addresses assessment and analysis of security control effectiveness and of organizational security status in accordance with organizational risk tolerance. Security control effectiveness is measured by correctness of implementation and by how adequately the implemented controls meet organizational needs in accordance with current risk tolerance (i.e., is the control implemented in accordance with the security plan to address threats and is the security plan adequate).[3] Organizational security status is determined using metrics established by the organization to best convey the security posture of an organization's information and information systems, along with organizational resilience given known threat information. This necessitates:

- Maintaining situational awareness of all systems across the organization;

- Maintaining an understanding of threats and threat activities;

- Assessing all security controls;

- Collecting, correlating, and analyzing security-related information;

- Providing actionable communication of security status across all tiers of the organization; and

- Active management of risk by organizational officials.

Communication with all stakeholders is key in developing the strategy and implementing the program. This document builds on the monitoring concepts introduced in NIST SP 800-37 Rev. 1, *Guide for Applying the Risk Management Framework to Federal Information Systems: A Security Life Cycle Approach.* An ISCM program helps to ensure that deployed security controls continue to be effective and that operations remain within stated organizational risk tolerances in light of the inevitable changes that occur over time. In cases where security controls are determined to be inadequate, ISCM programs facilitate prioritized security response actions based on risk.

An ISCM strategy is meaningful only within the context of broader organizational needs, objectives, or strategies, and as part of a broader risk management strategy, enabling timely

---

[2] The terms "continuous" and "ongoing" in this context mean that security controls and organizational risks are assessed and analyzed at a frequency sufficient to support risk-based security decisions to adequately protect organization information. Data collection, no matter how frequent, is performed at discrete intervals.

[3] NIST SP 800-53A, as amended, defines security control effectiveness as "the extent to which the controls are implemented correctly, operating as intended, and producing the desired outcome with respect to meeting the security requirements for the system."

management, assessment, and response to emerging security issues. Information collected through the ISCM program supports ongoing authorization decisions.[4]

ISCM, a critical step in an organization's Risk Management Framework (RMF), gives organizational officials access to security-related information on demand, enabling timely risk management decisions, including authorization decisions. Frequent updates to security plans, security assessment reports, plans of action and milestones, hardware and software inventories, and other system information are also supported. ISCM is most effective when automated mechanisms are employed where possible for data collection and reporting. Effectiveness is further enhanced when the output is formatted to provide information that is specific, measurable, actionable, relevant, and timely. While this document encourages the use of automation, it is recognized that many aspects of ISCM programs are not easily automated.

1.1 BACKGROUND

The concept of monitoring information system security has long been recognized as sound management practice. In 1997, Office of Management and Budget (OMB) Circular A-130, Appendix III[5] required agencies to *review* their information systems' security controls and to ensure that system changes do not have a significant impact on security, that security plans remain effective, and that security controls continue to perform as intended.

The Federal Information Security Management Act (FISMA) of 2002 further emphasized the importance of continuously monitoring information system security by requiring agencies to conduct assessments of security controls at a frequency appropriate to risk, but no less than annually.

Most recently, OMB issued memorandum M-11-33, *FY 2011 Reporting Instructions for the Federal Information Security Management Act and Agency Privacy Management*.[6] The memorandum provides instructions for annual FISMA reporting and emphasizes monitoring the security state of information systems on an ongoing basis with a frequency sufficient to make ongoing, risk-based decisions.

Tools supporting automated monitoring of some aspects of information systems have become an effective means for both data capture and data analysis. Ease of use, accessibility, and broad applicability across products and across vendors help to ensure that monitoring tools can be readily deployed in support of near real-time, risk-based decision making.

1.2 RELATIONSHIP TO OTHER SPECIAL PUBLICATIONS

NIST SP 800-39, *Managing Information Security Risk: Organization, Mission, and Information System View*, describes three key organization-wide ISCM activities: monitoring for effectiveness, monitoring for changes to systems and environments of operation, and monitoring

---

[4] See OMB Memoranda M-11-33, Question #28, for information on ongoing authorization
     (http://www.whitehouse.gov/sites/default/files/omb/memoranda/2011/m11-33.pdf).

[5] OMB Circular A-130 is available at http://www.whitehouse.gov/omb/circulars_a130_a130trans4.

[6] OMB memorandum M-11-33 is available at
     http://www.whitehouse.gov/sites/default/files/omb/memoranda/2011/m11-33.pdf.

for compliance. NIST SP 800-37 describes monitoring security controls at the system level (RMF Step 6) and also includes an organization-wide perspective, integration with the system development life cycle (SDLC), and support for ongoing authorizations. The concepts presented in NIST SP 800-39 and NIST SP 800-37 are expanded upon in order to provide guidelines sufficient for developing an ISCM strategy and implementing an ISCM program.

The tiered approach herein mirrors that described in NIST SP 800-37 and NIST SP 800-39 where Tier 1 is organization, Tier 2 is mission/business processes, and Tier 3 is information systems. In NIST SP 800-39, these tiers are used to address risk management from varying organizational perspectives. In this document, the tiers are used to address perspectives for ISCM for each tier. Organization-wide, tier-specific ISCM policies, procedures, and responsibilities are included for the organization, mission/business processes, and information systems tiers. Automation is leveraged where possible, and manual (e.g., procedural) monitoring methodologies are implemented where automation is not practical or possible.

The ISCM program will evolve over time as the program matures in general, additional tools and resources become available, measurement and automation capabilities mature, and changes are implemented to ensure continuous improvement in the organizational security posture and in the organization's security program. The monitoring strategy is regularly reviewed for relevance and accuracy in reflecting organizational risk tolerances, correctness of measurements, applicability of metrics, and effectiveness in supporting risk management decisions.

1.3 PURPOSE

The purpose of this guideline is to assist organizations in the development of an ISCM strategy and the implementation of an ISCM program that provides awareness of threats and vulnerabilities, visibility into organizational assets, and the effectiveness of deployed security controls. The ISCM strategy and program support ongoing assurance that planned and implemented security controls are aligned with organizational risk tolerance, as well as the ability to provide the information needed to respond to risk in a timely manner.

1.4 TARGET AUDIENCE

This publication serves individuals associated with the design, development, implementation, operation, maintenance, and disposal of federal information systems, including:

- Individuals with mission/business ownership responsibilities or fiduciary responsibilities (e.g., heads of federal agencies, chief executive officers, chief financial officers);

- Individuals with information system development and integration responsibilities (e.g., program managers, information technology product developers, information system developers, information systems integrators, enterprise architects, information security architects);

- Individuals with information system and/or security management/oversight responsibilities (e.g., senior leaders, risk executives, authorizing officials, chief information officers, senior information security officers[7]);

---

[7] At the *agency* level, this position is known as the Senior Agency Information Security Officer. Organizations may also refer to this position as the Chief Information Security Officer.

- Individuals with information system and security control assessment and monitoring responsibilities (e.g., system evaluators, assessors/assessment teams, independent verification and validation assessors, auditors, or information system owners); and

- Individuals with information security implementation and operational responsibilities (e.g., information system owners, common control providers, information owners/stewards, mission/business owners, information security architects, information system security engineers/officers).

1.5 ORGANIZATION OF THIS SPECIAL PUBLICATION

The remainder of this special publication is organized as follows:

- Chapter 2 describes the fundamentals of ongoing monitoring of information security in support of risk management;

- Chapter 3 describes the process of ISCM, including implementation guidelines; and

- Supporting appendices provide additional information regarding ISCM including: (A) general references; (B) definitions and terms; (C) acronyms; and (D) descriptions of technologies for enabling ISCM.

CHAPTER TWO

THE FUNDAMENTALS

ONGOING MONITORING IN SUPPORT OF RISK MANAGEMENT

This chapter describes the fundamental concepts associated with organization-wide continuous monitoring of information security and the application of ISCM in support of organizational risk management decisions (e.g., risk response decisions, ongoing system authorization decisions, Plans of Action and Milestones (POA&M) resource and prioritization decisions, etc.). In order to effectively address ever-increasing security challenges, a well-designed ISCM strategy addresses monitoring and assessment of security controls for effectiveness, and security status monitoring.[8] It also incorporates processes to assure that response actions are taken in accordance with findings and organizational risk tolerances and to assure that said responses have the intended effects.

The process of implementing ISCM as described in Chapter Three is:

• **Define** the ISCM strategy;

• **Establish** an ISCM program;

• **Implement** the ISCM program;

• **Analyze** and **Report** findings;

• **Respond** to findings; and

• **Review** and **Update** ISCM strategy and program.

ISCM strategies evolve in accordance with drivers for risk-based decision making and requirements for information. These requirements may come from any tier in the organization. Organizations implement ISCM based on requirements of those accountable and responsible for maintaining ongoing control of organizational security posture to within organizational risk tolerances. The implementation is standardized across the organization to the greatest extent possible so as to minimize use of resources (e.g., funding for purchase of tools/applications, data calls, organization-wide policies/procedures/templates, etc.) and to maximize leveragability of security-related information. Upon analysis, the resulting information informs the discrete processes used to manage the organization's security posture and overall risk. ISCM helps to provide situational awareness of the security status of the organization's systems based on information collected from resources (e.g., people, processes, technology, environment) and the capabilities in place to react as the situation changes.

---

[8] Organizations implement processes to manage organizational security and metrics that provide insight into those processes and hence into organizational security status. Some of those security processes will align with individual security controls, and others will align with components or combinations of controls. Discussions of metrics can be found in Section 3.2.1 and in NIST SP 800-55, *Performance Measurement Guide for Information Security,* as amended.

ISCM is a tactic in a larger strategy of organization-wide risk management.[9] Organizations increase situational awareness through enhanced monitoring capabilities and subsequently increase insight into and control of the processes used to manage organizational security. Increased insight into and control of security processes in turn enhances situational awareness. Therefore, the process of implementing ISCM is recursive. ISCM informs and is informed by distinct organizational security processes and associated requirements for input and output of security-related information. Consider the following example:

Security-related information pertaining to a system component inventory is used to determine compliance with CM-8 *Information System Component Inventory*.[10] The information is assessed to determine whether or not the control is effective, (i.e., if the inventory is accurate). If found to be inaccurate, an analysis to determine the root cause of the inaccuracy is initiated (e.g., perhaps a process for connecting components to the network has been ignored or is out of date, asset management tools are not operating as expected, or the organization is under attack). Based on the analysis, responses are initiated as appropriate (e.g., responsible parties update inventory, update relevant organizational processes, train employees, disconnect errant devices, etc.). Additionally, security-related information pertaining to a system component inventory may be used to support predefined metrics. More accurate system component inventories support improved effectiveness of other security domains such as patch management and vulnerability management.

This example illustrates how data collected in assessing a security control is leveraged to calculate a metric and provide input into various organizational processes. It further illustrates that a problem, once detected, can trigger an assessment of one or more controls across an organization, updates to relevant security-related information, modifications to the organizational security program plan and security processes, and improved compliance to the security program and applicable system security plan. The end result is improved organization-wide risk management and continual improvement limited only by the speed with which the organization can collect information and respond to findings.

2.1 ORGANIZATION-WIDE VIEW OF ISCM

Maintaining an up-to-date view of information security risks across an organization is a complex, multifaceted undertaking. It requires the involvement of the entire organization, from senior leaders providing governance and strategic vision to individuals developing, implementing, and operating individual information systems in support of the organization's core missions and business functions. Figure 2-1 illustrates a tiered approach to organization-wide ISCM in support of risk management. Tier 1 governance, risk management goals, and organizational risk tolerance drive the ISCM strategy. Organizational risk tolerance established by senior executives/leaders as part of the risk executive (function)[11] influences ISCM policy, procedures, and implementation activities across all tiers. Data collection primarily occurs at the information systems tier. Metrics are designed to present information in a context that is meaningful for each tier. For example, ISCM data collected at Tier 3 may be aggregated to provide security status or risk scores for a single system, for a collection of systems, across a core business process, or for the entire organization. Policies, procedures, and tools may be established at any tier; however, when

---

[9] ISCM is discussed within the larger context of organization-wide risk management in NIST SP 800-39.

[10] CM-8 is a security control from the Configuration Management family in NIST SP 800-53, Appendix F.

[11] See Section 2.4 for a discussion of roles and responsibilities of the risk executive (function).

established at Tiers 1 or 2, they facilitate the consistent implementation of ISCM across the organization and better support data reuse and judicious use of resources. Data collection, analysis, and reporting are automated where possible.[12] Through the use of automation, it is possible to monitor a greater number of security metrics with fewer resources, higher frequencies, larger sample sizes,[13] and with greater consistency and reliability than is feasible using manual processes. Organizations regularly review the ISCM strategy to ensure that metrics continue to be relevant, meaningful, actionable, and supportive of risk management decisions made by organizational officials at all tiers.

---

[12] Care must be taken in determining how best to use security-related information from individual information systems in calculating organizational metrics for security and risk. Dashboards and metrics, designed to provide organizational situational awareness of security and risk, can provide a false sense of security if used without continued assurance of the relevance of the metrics.

[13] If an organization does not have the resources or infrastructure necessary to assess every relevant object within its information infrastructure, sampling is an approach that may be useful in reducing the level of effort associated with continuous monitoring. Additional information is provided in Section 3.1.4.

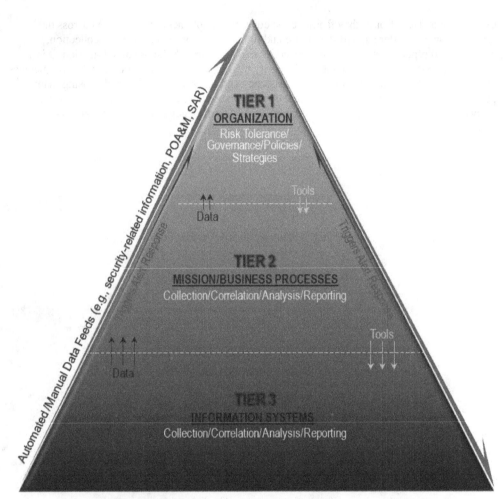

Figure 2-1. Organization-wide ISCM

An organization-wide approach to continuous monitoring of information and information system security supports risk-related decision making at the *organization* level (Tier 1), the *mission/business processes* level (Tier 2), and the *information systems* level (Tier 3).[14]

2.1.1 TIER 1- ORGANIZATION

Tier 1 risk management activities address high-level information security governance policy as it relates to risk to the organization as a whole, to its core missions, and to its business functions. At this tier, the criteria for ISCM are defined by the organization's risk management strategy, including how the organization plans to assess, respond to, and monitor risk, and the oversight required to ensure that the risk management strategy is effective. Security controls, security status, and other metrics defined and monitored by officials at this tier are designed to deliver information necessary to make risk management decisions in support of governance. Tier 1 metrics are developed for supporting governance decisions regarding the organization, its core missions, and

---

[14]   NIST Special Publication 800-39, as amended, provides guidelines on the holistic approach to risk management.

its business functions. Tier 1 metrics may be calculated based on security-related information from common, hybrid, and system-specific security controls. The metrics and the frequency with which they are monitored[15] and reported are determined by requirements to maintain operations within organizational risk tolerances. As part of the overall governance structure established by the organization, the Tier 1 risk management strategy and the associated monitoring requirements are communicated throughout Tiers 2 and 3.

2.1.2 TIER 2 - MISSION/BUSINESS PROCESSES

Organizational officials that are accountable for one or more missions or business processes are also responsible for overseeing the associated risk management activities for those processes. The Tier 2 criteria for continuous monitoring of information security are defined by how core mission/business processes are prioritized with respect to the overall goals and objectives of the organization, the types of information needed to successfully execute the stated mission/business processes, and the organization-wide information security program strategy. Controls in the Program Management (PM) family are an example of Tier 2 security controls. These controls address the establishment and management of the organization's information security program. Tier 2 controls are deployed organization-wide and support all information systems. They may be tracked at Tier 2 or Tier 1. The frequencies with which Tier 2 security controls are assessed and security status and other metrics are monitored are determined in part by the objectives and priorities of the mission or business process and measurement capabilities inherent in the infrastructure.[16] Security-related information may come from common, hybrid, and system-specific controls. Metrics and dashboards can be useful at Tiers 1 and 2 in assessing, normalizing, communicating, and correlating monitoring activities below the mission/business processes tier in a meaningful manner.

2.1.3 TIER 3 - INFORMATION SYSTEMS

ISCM activities at Tier 3 address risk management from an *information system* perspective. These activities include ensuring that all system-level security controls (technical, operational, and management controls) are implemented correctly, operate as intended, produce the desired outcome with respect to meeting the security requirements for the system, and continue to be effective over time. ISCM activities at Tier 3 also include assessing and monitoring hybrid and common controls implemented at the system level. Security status reporting at this tier often includes but is not limited to security alerts, security incidents, and identified threat activities.[17] The ISCM strategy for Tier 3 also ensures that security-related information supports the monitoring requirements of other organizational tiers. Data feeds/assessment results from system-level controls (system-specific, hybrid, or common), along with associated security status reporting, support risk-based decisions at the organization and mission/business processes tiers. Information is tailored for each tier and delivered in ways that inform risk-based decision making at all tiers. Those resulting decisions impact the ISCM strategy applied at the information systems tier.[18] ISCM metrics originating at the information systems tier can be used to assess, respond,

---

[15] Monitoring organizationally defined metrics is referred to as security status monitoring throughout this document.

[16] As an organization's technical and human capital capabilities mature, monitoring capabilities increase.

[17] Threat activities include malicious activities observed on organizational networks or other anomalous activities that are indicators of inappropriate actions. See NIST SP 800-30, as amended, for more information on threats.

[18] A continuous monitoring strategy for an individual system may also include metrics related to its potential impact on other systems.

and monitor risk across the organization. The ongoing monitoring activities implemented at the information systems tier provide security-related information to authorizing officials (AOs) in support of ongoing system authorization decisions and to the risk executive (function) in support of ongoing organizational risk management.

At Tier 3, RMF Step 6 Monitor activities and ISCM activities are closely aligned. The assessment methods relevant for implemented security controls are the same whether the assessments are being done solely in support of system authorization or in support of a broader, more comprehensive continuous monitoring effort. Information systems tier officials and staff conduct assessments and monitoring, and analyze results on an ongoing basis. The information is leveraged at the organization, mission/business processes, and information systems tiers to support risk management. Though frequency requirements differ, each tier receives the benefit of security-related information that is current and applicable to affected processes. RMF Step 6 activities performed within the context of an ISCM program support information system risk determination and acceptance, i.e., authorization (RMF Step 5) on an ongoing basis.

2.2   ONGOING SYSTEM AUTHORIZATIONS

Initial authorization to operate is based on evidence available at one point in time, but systems and environments of operation change. Ongoing assessment of security control effectiveness supports a system's security authorization over time in highly dynamic environments of operation with changing threats, vulnerabilities, technologies, and missions/business processes. Through ISCM, new threat or vulnerability information is evaluated as it becomes available, permitting organizations to make adjustments to security requirements or individual controls as needed to maintain authorization decisions. The process for obtaining system authorization, and more generally, for managing information security and information system-related risk, is the RMF.[19] The RMF, illustrated in Figure 2-2, provides a disciplined and structured process that integrates information system security and risk management activities into the SDLC. The monitoring step (Step 6) of the RMF includes interactions between the three tiers as illustrated in the organizational view of ISCM in Figure 2-1. Interaction between the tiers includes data from system owners, common control providers, and authorizing officials on security control assessments and ongoing authorization of system and common controls provided to the risk executive (function).[20] There is also dissemination of updated risk-related information such as vulnerability and threat data and organizational risk tolerance from Tiers 1 and 2 to authorizing officials and information system owners. When the RMF is applied within an organization that has also implemented a robust ISCM strategy, organizational officials are provided with a view of the organizational security posture and each system's contribution to said posture on demand.

---

[19] System authorization to operate may be partially dependent on assessment/monitoring and ongoing security authorization of common controls. NIST SP 800-37, as amended, provides information on security authorization of common controls.

[20] Roles and responsibilities of organizational officials within a continuous monitoring program are discussed in Section 2.4. NIST SP 800-37, as amended, describes the interaction of the risk executive (function) in the context of the RMF.

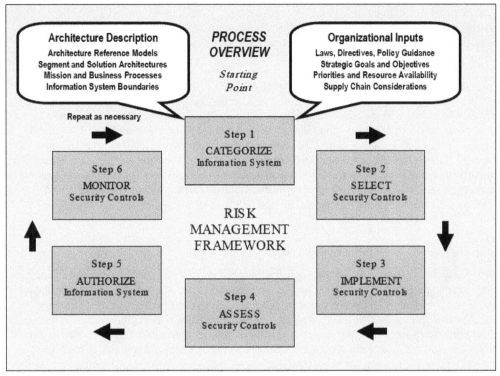

Figure 2-2. Risk Management Framework

The output of a strategically designed and well-managed organization-wide ISCM program can
be used to maintain a system's authorization to operate and keep required system information and
data (i.e., System Security Plan together with Risk Assessment Report, Security Assessment
Report, and POA&M) up to date on an ongoing basis. Security management and reporting tools
may provide functionality to automate updates to key evidence needed for ongoing authorization
decisions. ISCM also facilitates risk-based decision making regarding the ongoing authorization
to operate information systems and security authorization for common controls by providing
evolving threat activity or vulnerability information on demand. A security control assessment
and risk determination process, otherwise static between authorizations, is thus transformed into a
dynamic process that supports timely risk response actions and cost-effective, ongoing
authorizations. Continuous monitoring of threats, vulnerabilities, and security control
effectiveness provides situational awareness for risk-based support of ongoing authorization
decisions. An appropriately designed ISCM strategy and program supports ongoing authorization
of type authorizations, as well as single, joint, and leveraged authorizations.[21]

ISCM in support of ongoing assessment and authorization has the potential to be resource-
intensive and time-consuming. It is impractical to collect security-related information and assess
every aspect of every security control deployed across an organization at all times. A more
practical approach is to establish reasonable assessment frequencies for collecting security-related
information. The frequency of assessments should be sufficient to assure adequate security
commensurate with risk, as determined by system categorization and ISCM strategy

---

[21] See NIST SP 800-37, as amended, for a discussion of authorization types.

requirements. Sampling of information system security objects, rather than 100 percent inspection, can also be an efficient and effective means of monitoring, particularly in cases where monitoring is not automated. Important considerations in determining sample sizes and monitoring frequencies are discussed in Chapter Three.

Monitoring frequencies (e.g., annually, quarterly, monthly, daily) are not static, and they are not uniform across all metrics. Security control assessment and monitoring frequencies, for example, are adjusted to support changes in organizational information systems or their environments of operation, including emerging information on security threats and vulnerabilities. The priorities for ISCM vary and are adjusted in response to security incidents, to identify problems with security control implementations, or to evaluate changes to systems and system components that are determined to have a significant impact on security. An ISCM strategy can deliver dynamic updates of security-related data to support system authorizations conducted at any interval. Section 3.2.2 includes a more complete discussion of factors to consider when determining monitoring frequencies.

2.3   ROLE OF AUTOMATION IN ISCM

When possible, organizations look for automated solutions to lower costs, enhance efficiency, and improve the reliability of monitoring security-related information. Security is implemented through a combination of people, processes, and technology. The automation of information security deals primarily with automating aspects of security that require little human interaction. Automated tools are often able to recognize patterns and relationships that may escape the notice of human analysts, especially when the analysis is performed on large volumes of data. This includes items such as verifying technical settings on individual network endpoints or ensuring that the software on a machine is up to date with organizational policy. Automation serves to augment the security processes conducted by security professionals within an organization and may reduce the amount of time a security professional must spend on doing redundant tasks, thereby increasing the amount of time the trained professional may spend on tasks requiring human cognition.

The ISCM strategy does not focus solely on the security-related information that is easy for an organization to collect or easy to automate. When an ISCM program is first implemented, there will likely be several aspects of the organization's security program that are manually monitored. Organizations' monitoring capabilities will expand and mature over time. Metrics will evolve with lessons learned and with increased insight into organizational security status and risk tolerance. The focus of an ISCM strategy is to provide adequate information about security control effectiveness and organizational security status allowing organizational officials to make informed, timely security risk management decisions. Thus, implementation, effectiveness, and adequacy of all security controls are monitored along with organizational security status.

When determining the extent to which the organization automates ISCM, organizations consider potential efficiencies of process standardization that may be gained with automation, and the potential value (or lack of value) of the automated security-related information from a risk management perspective. Additionally, organizations consider intangibles such as the potential value of personnel reassignment and more comprehensive situational awareness.

While automation of IT security has the potential to significantly reduce the amount of time a human must spend doing certain tasks, it is not possible to fully automate all of an organization's information security program functions. The technologies discussed in Appendix D, for example, still require human analysis for implementation and maintenance of the tools as well as appropriate interpretation of findings. Similarly, these tools operate within the context of processes designed, run, and maintained by humans. If individuals carry out their responsibilities insecurely, then the effectiveness of the technologies is compromised, and the security of the systems and the mission/business or organizational processes supported by those systems is put in jeopardy.

Automation makes security-related information readily available in an environment where ongoing monitoring needs change. Therefore, during security control implementation (RMF Step 3), consideration is given to the capabilities inherent in available technology to support ISCM as part of the criteria in determining how best to implement a given control.

Consideration is given to ISCM tools that:

- Pull information from a variety of sources (i.e., assessment objects[22]);

- Use open specifications such as the Security Content Automation Protocol (SCAP);

- Offer interoperability with other products such as help desk, inventory management, configuration management, and incident response solutions;

- Support compliance with applicable federal laws, Executive Orders, directives, policies, regulations, standards, and guidelines;

- Provide reporting with the ability to tailor output and drill down from high-level, aggregate metrics to system-level metrics; and

- Allow for data consolidation into Security Information and Event Management (SIEM) tools and dashboard products.

Automation supports collecting more data more frequently and from a larger and more diverse pool of technologies, people, processes, and environments. It can therefore make comprehensive, ongoing control of information security practical and affordable. How effective the organization is in utilizing the monitoring results (obtained in a manual or automated fashion) still depends upon the organizational ISCM strategy, including validity and comprehensiveness of the metrics, as well as the processes in place to analyze monitoring results and respond to findings. Technologies for enabling automation of some ISCM tasks are discussed in greater detail in Appendix D.

2.4 ISCM ROLES AND RESPONSIBILITIES

This section describes the roles and responsibilities of key participants involved in an organization's ISCM program. Widely varying missions and organizational structures may lead to differences in naming conventions for ISCM-related roles and how specific responsibilities are allocated among organizational personnel (e.g., multiple individuals filling a single role or one

---

[22] See NIST SP 800-53A, as amended, for information on assessment objects.

individual filling multiple roles). Roles and responsibilities commonly associated with ISCM include:

Head of Agency. The agency head is likely to participate in the organization's ISCM program within the context of the risk executive (function).

Risk Executive (Function). The risk executive (function) oversees the organization's ISCM strategy and program. The risk executive (function) reviews status reports from the ISCM process as input to information security risk posture and risk tolerance decisions and provides input to mission/business process and information systems tier entities on ISCM strategy and requirements; promotes collaboration and cooperation among organizational entities; facilitates sharing of security-related information; provides an organization-wide forum to consider all sources of risk; and ensures that risk information is considered for continuous monitoring decisions.

Chief Information Officer (CIO). The CIO leads the organization's ISCM program. The CIO ensures that an effective ISCM program is established and implemented for the organization by establishing expectations and requirements for the organization's ISCM program; working closely with authorizing officials to provide funding, personnel, and other resources to support ISCM; and maintaining high-level communications and working group relationships among organizational entities.

Senior Information Security Officer (SISO). The SISO establishes, implements, and maintains the organization's ISCM program; develops organizational program guidance (i.e., policies/procedures) for continuous monitoring of the security program and information systems; develops configuration management guidance for the organization; consolidates and analyzes POA&Ms to determine organizational security weaknesses and deficiencies; acquires or develops and maintains automated tools to support ISCM and ongoing authorizations; provides training on the organization's ISCM program and process; and provides support to information owners/information system owners and common control providers on how to implement ISCM for their information systems.

Authorizing Official (AO). The AO assumes responsibility for ensuring the organization's ISCM program is applied with respect to a given information system. The AO ensures the security posture of the information system is maintained, reviews security status reports and critical security documents and determines if the risk to the organization from operation of the information system remains acceptable. The AO also determines whether significant information system changes require reauthorization actions and reauthorizes the information system when required.

Information System Owner (ISO)/Information Owner/Steward. The ISO establishes processes and procedures in support of system-level implementation of the organization's ISCM program. This includes developing and documenting an ISCM strategy for the information system; participating in the organization's configuration management process; establishing and maintaining an inventory of components associated with the information system; conducting security impact analyses on changes to the information system; conducting, or ensuring conduct of, assessment of security controls according to the ISCM strategy; preparing and submitting security status reports in accordance with organizational policy and procedures; conducting remediation activities as necessary to maintain system authorization; revising the system-level security control monitoring process as required; reviewing ISCM reports from common control providers to verify that the common controls continue to provide adequate protection for the information system; and updating critical security documents based on the results of ISCM.

Common Control Provider. [23] The common control provider establishes processes and procedures in support of ongoing monitoring of common controls. The common control provider develops and documents an ISCM strategy for assigned common controls; participates in the organization's configuration management process; establishes and maintains an inventory of components associated with the common controls; conducts security impact analyses on changes that affect the common controls; ensures security controls are assessed according to the ISCM strategy; prepares and submits security status reports in accordance with organizational policy/procedures; conducts remediation activities as necessary to maintain common control authorization; updates/revises the common security control monitoring process as required; updates critical security documents as changes occur; and distributes critical security documents to individual information owners/information system owners, and other senior leaders in accordance with organizational policy/procedures.

Information System Security Officer (ISSO). The ISSO supports the organization's ISCM program by assisting the ISO in completing ISCM responsibilities and by participating in the configuration management process.

Security Control Assessor. The security control assessor provides input into the types of security-related information gathered as part of ISCM and assesses information system or program management security controls for the organization's ISCM program. The security control assessor develops a security assessment plan for each security control; submits the security assessment plan for approval prior to conducting assessments; conducts assessments of security controls as defined in the security assessment plan; updates the security assessment report as changes occur during ISCM; and updates/revises the security assessment plan as needed.

Organizations may define other roles (e.g., information system administrator, ISCM program manager) as needed to support the ISCM process.

---

[23]   Organizations may have multiple common control providers.

CHAPTER THREE

THE PROCESS

Defining an ISCM Strategy and Implementing an ISCM Program

This chapter describes the process for developing an ISCM strategy and implementing an ISCM program including activities at the organization, mission/business process, and information systems tiers. A well-designed ISCM strategy encompasses security control assessment, security status monitoring, and security status reporting in support of timely risk-based decision making throughout the organization. It also incorporates processes to assure that response actions are taken. An organization's strategy for action based on the data collected is as important (if not more important) than collecting the data. The process for developing an ISCM strategy and implementing an ISCM program is as follows:

- **Define** an ISCM strategy based on risk tolerance that maintains clear visibility into assets, awareness of vulnerabilities, up-to-date threat information, and mission/business impacts.

- **Establish** an ISCM program determining metrics, status monitoring frequencies, control assessment frequencies, and an ISCM technical architecture.

- **Implement** an ISCM program and collect the security-related information required for metrics, assessments, and reporting. Automate collection, analysis, and reporting of data where possible.

- **Analyze** the data collected and **Report** findings, determining the appropriate response. It may be necessary to collect additional information to clarify or supplement existing monitoring data.

- **Respond** to findings with technical, management, and operational mitigating activities or acceptance, transference/sharing, or avoidance/rejection.

- **Review and Update** the monitoring program, adjusting the ISCM strategy and maturing measurement capabilities to increase visibility into assets and awareness of vulnerabilities, further enable data-driven control of the security of an organization's information infrastructure, and increase organizational resilience.

This process is depicted below in Figure 3- 1.

Figure 3-1. ISCM Process

Risk tolerance, enterprise architecture, security architecture, security configurations, plans for
changes to the enterprise architecture, and available threat information provide data that is
fundamental to the execution of these steps and to ongoing management of information security-
related risks. Security-related information is analyzed for its relevance to organizational risk
management at all three tiers.

The balance of this chapter discusses the process of ISCM, providing detail on topics not covered
by existing guidelines and referencing existing guidelines where appropriate. Primary roles,
supporting roles, expected inputs, and expected outputs are given for each process step as a guide.
Roles and responsibilities will vary across organizations as will implementation-level details of
an ISCM program.

3.1 DEFINE ISCM STRATEGY

Effective ISCM begins with development of a strategy that addresses ISCM requirements and
activities at each organizational tier (organization, mission/business processes, and information
systems). Each tier monitors security metrics and assesses security control effectiveness with
established monitoring and assessment frequencies and status reports customized to support tier-
specific decision making. Policies, procedures, tools, and templates that are implemented from
Tiers 1 and 2, or that are managed in accordance with guidance from Tiers 1 and 2, best support
shared use of data within and across tiers. The lower tiers may require information in addition to
that required at higher tiers and hence develop tier-specific strategies that are consistent with
those at higher tiers and still sufficient to address local tier requirements for decision making.
Depending on the organization, there may be overlap in the tasks and activities conducted at each
tier.

The guidelines below, though not prescriptive, helps to ensure an organization-wide approach to
ISCM that best promotes standardized methodologies and consistent practices and hence

maximizes efficiencies and leveragability of security-related data. As changes occur, the ISCM strategy is reviewed for relevance, accuracy in reflecting organizational risk tolerances, correctness of measurements, and applicability of metrics. An inherent part of any ISCM strategy is the inclusion of criteria describing the conditions that trigger a review or update of the strategy, in addition to the preestablished frequency audit. Likewise, the organization defines criteria and procedures for updating the ISCM program based on the revised ISCM strategy.

3.1.1 ORGANIZATION (TIER 1) AND MISSION/BUSINESS PROCESSES (TIER 2) ISCM STRATEGY

The risk executive (function) determines the overall organizational risk tolerance and risk mitigation strategy at the organization tier.[24] The ISCM strategy is developed and implemented to support risk management in accordance with organizational risk tolerance. While ISCM strategy, policy, and procedures may be developed at any tier, typically, the organization-wide ISCM strategy and associated policy are developed at the organization tier with general procedures for implementation developed at the mission/business processes tier. If the organization-wide strategy is developed at the mission/business processes tier, Tier 1 officials review and approve the strategy to ensure that organizational risk tolerance across all missions and business processes has been appropriately considered. This information is communicated to staff at the mission/business processes and information systems tiers and reflected in mission/business processes and information systems tier strategy, policy, and procedures.

When developed at Tiers 1 and/or 2, the following policies, procedures, and templates facilitate organization-wide, standardized processes in support of the ISCM strategy:

- Policy that defines key metrics;

- Policy for modifications to and maintenance of the monitoring strategy;

- Policy and procedures for the assessment of security control effectiveness (common, hybrid, and system-level controls);

- Policy and procedures for security status monitoring;

- Policy and procedures for security status reporting (on control effectiveness and status monitoring);

- Policy and procedures for assessing risks and gaining threat information and insights;

- Policy and procedures for configuration management and security impact analysis;[25]

- Policy and procedures for implementation and use of organization-wide tools;

- Policy and procedures for establishment of monitoring frequencies;

- Policy and procedures for determining sample sizes and populations and for managing object sampling;

- Procedures for determining security metrics and data sources;

---

[24]   See NIST SP 800-39, as amended, for a discussion of the risk executive (function) roles and responsibilities.

[25]   See NIST SP 800-128, as amended, for more information on security-focused configuration management.

- Templates for assessing risks; and

- Templates for security status reporting (on control effectiveness and status monitoring).

Policy, procedures, and templates necessarily address manual and automated monitoring methodologies. Additionally at these tiers, organizations establish policy and procedures for training of personnel with ISCM roles. This may include training on management and use of automated tools (e.g., establishing baselines and tuning of measurements to provide accurate monitoring of operational environments). It may also include training for recognition of and appropriate response to triggers and alerts from metrics indicating risks beyond acceptable limits, as well as training on internal or external reporting requirements. This training may be included in existing role-based training requirements for those with significant security roles, or it may consist of training specifically focused on implementation of the organization's ISCM policy and procedures.

When implementing policies, procedures, and templates developed at higher tiers, lower tiers fill in any gaps related to their tier-specific processes. Decisions and activities by Tier 1 and 2 officials may be constrained by things such as mission/business needs, limitations of the infrastructure (including the human components), immutable governance policies, and external drivers.

Primary Roles: Risk Executive (Function), Chief Information Officer, Senior Information Security Officer, Authorizing Officials

Supporting Roles: Information System Owner/Common Control Provider

Expected Input: Organizational risk assessment and current risk tolerance, current threat information, organizational expectations and priorities, available tools from OMB lines of business and/or third-party vendors

Expected Output: Updated information on organizational risk tolerance, organization-wide ISCM strategy and associated policy, procedures, templates, tools

3.1.2 INFORMATION SYSTEM (TIER 3) ISCM STRATEGY

The system-level ISCM strategy is developed and implemented to support risk management, not only at the information systems tier, but at *all three tiers* in accordance with system and organizational risk tolerance. Although the strategy may be defined at Tiers 1 or 2, system-specific policy and procedures for implementation may also be developed at Tier 3. System-level security-related information includes assessment data *pertaining to* system-level security controls and metrics data *obtained from* system-level security controls. System owners establish a system-level strategy for ISCM by considering factors such as the system's architecture and operational environment, as well as organizational and mission-level requirements,[26] policy, procedures, and templates.

System-level ISCM addresses monitoring security controls for effectiveness (assessments), monitoring for security status, and reporting findings. At a minimum, all security controls, including common and hybrid controls implemented at the system level, are assessed for

---

[26] The ISCM strategy is designed, in part, to help ensure that compromises to the security architecture are managed in a way to prevent or minimize impact on business and mission functions.

effectiveness in accordance with the system security plan and the methods described in NIST SP 800-53A, as amended. System owners determine assessment frequencies of security controls based on drivers from all three tiers. A full discussion of factors to consider when determining assessment and monitoring frequencies can be found in Section 3.2.2. System-level security-related information is used to determine security status at all three tiers. Use of system-level security-related information in metrics for determining security status is addressed in Section 3.2.1.

The ISCM strategy at the information systems tier also supports ongoing authorization. Ongoing authorization implies recurring updates to the authorization decision information in accordance with assessment and monitoring frequencies. Assessment results from monitoring common controls implemented and managed at the organization or mission/business process tier may be combined with information generated at the information systems tier in order to provide the authorizing official (AO) with a complete set of independently-generated evidence.[27] Assessment evidence obtained from ISCM is, at a minimum, provided to AOs as often as required by organizational policy.

Primary Roles: Information System Owner/Common Control Provider, Information System Security Officer

Supporting Roles: Senior Information Security Officer, Authorizing Official, Security Control Assessor

Expected Input: Organizational risk tolerance information, organizational ISCM strategy, policy, procedures, templates, system-specific threat information, and system information (e.g., System Security Plan, Security Assessment Report, Plan of Action and Milestones, Security Assessment Plan, System Risk Assessment, etc.[28])

Expected Output: System-level ISCM strategy that complements the Tier 1 and 2 strategies and the organizational security program and that provides security status information for all tiers and real-time updates for ongoing system authorization decisions as directed by the organizational ISCM strategy

3.1.3 PROCESS ROLES AND RESPONSIBILITIES

Tiers 1 and 2 officials have responsibilities throughout the ISCM process, including, but not limited to, the following:

- Provide input to the development of the organizational ISCM strategy including establishment of metrics, policy, and procedures, compiling and correlating Tier 3 data into security-related information of use at Tiers 1 and 2, policies on assessment and monitoring frequencies, and provisions for ensuring sufficient depth and coverage when sampling methodologies are utilized [ISCM steps: Define, Establish, Implement].

---

[27] See NIST SP 800-53, CA-2, Control Enhancement 1, for specific assessor independence requirements. Assessors need only be independent of the operation of the system. They may be from within the organizational tier, the mission/business tier, or from within some other independent entity internal or external to the organization. Results of assessments done by system operators can be used if they have been validated by independent assessors.

[28] This system information is an outcome of the RMF. Electronic standardized templates and document management systems readily support frequent updates with data generated by continuous monitoring programs.

- Review monitoring results (security-related information) to determine security status in accordance with organizational policy and definitions [ISCM step: Analyze/Report].

- Analyze potential security impact to organization and mission/business process functions resulting from changes to information systems and their environments of operation, along with the security impact to the enterprise architecture resulting from the addition or removal of information systems [ISCM step: Analyze/Report].

- Make a determination as to whether or not current risk is within organizational risk tolerance levels [ISCM steps: Analyze/Report, Review/Update].

- Take steps to respond to risk as needed (e.g., request new or revised metrics, additional or revised assessments, modifications to existing common or PM security controls, or additional controls) based on the results of ongoing monitoring activities and assessment of risk [ISCM step: Respond].

- Update relevant security documentation [ISCM step: Respond].

- Review new or modified legislation, directives, policies, etc., for any changes to security requirements [ISCM step: Review/Update].

- Review monitoring results to determine if organizational plans and polices should be adjusted or updated [ISCM step: Review/Update].

- Review monitoring results to identify new information on vulnerabilities [ISCM step: Review/Update].

- Review information on new or emerging threats as evidenced by threat activities present in monitoring results, threat modeling (asset- and attack-based), classified and unclassified threat briefs, USCERT reports, and other information available through trusted sources, interagency sharing, and external government sources [ISCM step: Review/Update].

Tier 3 officials have responsibilities throughout the ISCM process including, but not limited to, the following:

- Provide input to the development and implementation of the organization-wide ISCM strategy along with development and implementation of the system level ISCM strategy [ISCM steps: Define, Establish, Implement; RMF Step: Select].

- Support planning and implementation of security controls, the deployment of automation tools, and how those tools interface with one another in support of the ISCM strategy [ISCM step: Implement; RMF Step: Select].

- Determine the security impact of changes to the information system and its environment of operation, including changes associated with commissioning or decommissioning the system [ISCM step: Analyze/Report; RMF Step: Monitor].

- Assess ongoing security control effectiveness [ISCM step: Implement; RMF Steps: Assess,[29] Monitor].

- Take steps to respond to risk as needed (e.g., request additional or revised assessments, modify existing security controls, implement additional security controls, accept risk, etc.) based on the results of ongoing monitoring activities, assessment of risk, and outstanding items in the plan of action and milestones [ISCM step: Respond; RMF Step: Monitor].

- Provide ongoing input to the security plan, security assessment report, and plan of action and milestones based on the results of the ISCM process [ISCM step: Respond; RMF Step: 6].

- Report the security status of the information system including the data needed to inform Tiers 1 and 2 metrics [ISCM step: Analyze/Report; RMF Steps: Assess, Monitor].

- Review the reported security status of the information system to determine whether the risk to the system and the organization remains within organizational risk tolerances [ISCM step: Analyze/Report; RMF Steps: Authorize, Monitor].

3.1.4 DEFINE SAMPLE POPULATIONS

Organizations may find that collecting data from every object of every system within an organization may be impractical or cost-prohibitive. Sampling is a methodology employable with both manual and automated monitoring that may make ISCM more cost-effective. A risk with sampling is that the sample population may fail to capture the variations in assessment outcomes that would be obtained from an assessment of the full population. This could result in an inaccurate view of security control effectiveness and organizational security status.

NIST SP 800-53A, as amended, describes how to achieve satisfactory coverage when determining sample populations for the three named assessment methods: examine, interview, and test. The guidelines in NIST SP 800-53A for basic, focused, and comprehensive testing[30] addresses the need for a "representative sample of assessment objects" or a "sufficiently large sample of assessment objects." Statistical tools can be used to help quantify sample size.

NIST 800-53A provides guidelines to help address the general issue of sampling and particularly that of coverage. In selecting a sample population, the coverage attribute is satisfied through consideration of three criteria:

- **Types of objects** - ensure sufficient diversity of types of assessment objects;

- **Number of each type** - chose "enough" objects of each type to provide confidence that assessment of additional objects will result in consistent findings; and

- **Specific objects per type assessed** - given all of the objects of relevance throughout the organization that could be assessed, include "enough" objects per type in the sample population to sufficiently account for the known or anticipated variance in assessment outcomes.

---

[29] Prior to initial authorization, the system is not included in the organization's continuous monitoring program. This reference to RMF 4 is relevant after the system becomes operational, and is passing through Step 4 in support of ongoing authorization.

[30] See NIST SP 800-53A, as amended, Appendix D.

Sample measurements are summarized into a statistic (e.g., sample mean) and the observed value compared with the allowable value as represented by organizational risk tolerance. Statistics calculated using sampling can become less reliable predictors of the full population if the population is not randomly selected and if the sample size (i.e., objects to be tested) is small.[31] As described in the NIST Engineering Statistics Handbook, when deciding how many objects to include in sample populations, the following are considered:[32]

- Desired information (what question will the measurements help answer);

- Cost and practicality of making the assessment;

- Information already known about the objects, organization, or operating environments;

- Anticipated variability across the total population; and

- Desired confidence in resulting statistics and conclusions drawn about the total population.

Ways to achieve "increased" or "further increased grounds for confidence that a control is implemented correctly and operating as intended" across the entire organization include asking more targeted questions, increasing the types of objects assessed, and increasing the number of each type of object assessed.

Organizations may also target specific objects for assessment in addition to the random sample, using the above criteria. However, sampling methods other than random sampling are used with care to avoid introducing bias. Automated data collection and analysis can reduce the need for sampling.

Primary Roles: Information System Owner, Common Control Provider, Information System Security Officer, Security Control Assessor

Supporting Roles: Risk Executive (Function), Authorizing Official, Chief Information Officer, Senior Information Security Officer

Expected Input: Organizational- and system-level policy and procedures on ISCM strategy, metrics, and the Security Assessment Plan updated with assessment and monitoring frequencies

Expected Output: Security Assessment Plan documentation on acceptable sample sizes, security-related information

---

[31] The Central Limit Theorem is a key theorem that allows one to assume that a statistic (e.g., mean) calculated from a random sample has a normal distribution (i.e., bell curve) regardless of the underlying distribution from which individual samples are being taken. For small sample sizes (roughly less than 30), the normal distribution assumption tends to be good only if the underlying distribution from which random samples are being taken is close to normal.

[32] For detailed information on selecting sample sizes, see http://www.itl.nist.gov/div898/handbook/ppc/section3/ppc333.htm.

3.2 ESTABLISH AN ISCM PROGRAM

Organizations establish a program to implement the ISCM strategy. The program is sufficient to inform risk-based decisions and maintain operations within established risk tolerances. Goals include detection of anomalies and changes in the organization's environments of operation and information systems, visibility into assets, awareness of vulnerabilities, knowledge of threats, security control effectiveness, and security status including compliance. Metrics are designed and frequencies determined to ensure that information needed to manage risk to within organizational risk tolerances is available. Tools, technologies, and manual and/or automated methodologies are implemented within the context of an architecture designed to deliver the required information in the appropriate context and at the right frequencies.

3.2.1 DETERMINE METRICS

Organizations determine metrics to be used to evaluate and control ongoing risk to the organization. Metrics, which include all the security-related information from assessments and monitoring produced by automated tools and manual procedures, are organized into meaningful information to support decision making and reporting requirements. Metrics should be derived from specific objectives that will maintain or improve security posture. Metrics are developed for system-level data to make it meaningful in the context of mission/business or organizational risk management.

Metrics may use security-related information acquired at different frequencies and therefore with varying data latencies. Metrics may be calculated from a combination of security status monitoring, security control assessment data, and from data collected from one or more security controls. Metrics may be determined at any tier or across an organization. Some examples of metrics are the number and severity of vulnerabilities revealed and remediated, number of unauthorized access attempts, configuration baseline information, contingency plan testing dates and results, and number of employees who are current on awareness training requirements. risk tolerance thresholds for organizations, and the risk score associated with a given system configuration.

As an example, a metric that an organization might use to monitor status of authorized and unauthorized components on a network could rely on related metrics such as physical asset locations, logical asset locations (subnets/Internet protocol (IP) addresses), media access control (MAC) addresses, system association, and policies/procedures for network connectivity. The metrics would be refreshed at various frequencies in accordance with the ISCM strategy. The metrics might be computed hourly, daily, or weekly. Though logical asset information might change daily, it is likely that policies and procedures for network connectivity will be reviewed or revised no more than annually. These metrics are informative only and are not recommended metrics. They are included to assist in explaining the concept of metrics as they are applied across tiers. Organizations define their own metrics and associated monitoring frequencies. In order to calculate metrics, associated controls and/or their objects are assessed and monitored with frequencies consistent with the timing requirements expressed in the metric.

It should be noted that metrics are fundamentally flawed without assurance that *all* security controls are implemented correctly. Metrics are defined or calculated in accordance with output from the security architecture. Collecting metrics from a security architecture with security controls that have not been assessed is equivalent to using a broken or uncalibrated scale. The interpretation of metrics data presumes that controls directly and indirectly used in the metric calculation are implemented and working as anticipated. If a metric indicates a problem, the root cause could be any number of things. Without fundamental assurance of correct implementation and continued effectiveness of security controls that are *not* associated with the metric, the root cause analysis is going to be hampered, and the analysis may be inappropriately narrowed to a predetermined list, overlooking the true problem. For detailed information on establishing metrics, see NIST SP 800-55, as amended.

Primary Roles: Risk Executive (Function), Chief Information Officer, Senior Information Security Officer

Supporting Roles: Authorizing Officials, Information System Owner/Common Control Provider

Expected Input: Organizational risk assessment, organizational risk tolerance, current threat information, reporting requirements, current vulnerability information

Expected Output: Established metrics to convey security status and security control effectiveness at all three tiers, and to give recipients/users of reports visibility into assets, awareness of vulnerabilities, and knowledge of threats

3.2.2 ESTABLISH MONITORING AND ASSESSMENT FREQUENCIES

Determining frequencies for security status monitoring and for security control assessments are critical functions of the organization's ISCM program. For some organizations, dashboards and ongoing assessments are a shift away from the model of complete security control assessments conducted at a distinct point in time. For this shift to be constructive and effective from security, assurance, and resource use perspectives, organizations determine the frequencies with which *each* security control or control element is assessed for effectiveness and the frequencies with which *each* metric is monitored.

Security control effectiveness across a tier or throughout the organization can itself be taken as a security metric and as such may have an associated status monitoring frequency. Though monitoring and assessment frequencies are determined for each individual metric and control, organizations use this data of different latencies to create a holistic view of the security of each system as well as a view of the security of the enterprise architecture. As the monitoring program matures, monitoring and assessment frequencies are important in the context of how the data is used and the question *When did the system receive authorization to operate?* will become less meaningful than *How resilient is the system?*

Considerations in Determining Assessment and Monitoring Frequencies.

Organizations take the following criteria into consideration when establishing monitoring frequencies for metrics or assessment frequencies for security controls:

- **Security control volatility**. Volatile security controls are assessed more frequently, whether the objective is establishing security control effectiveness or supporting calculation of a metric.[33] Controls in the NIST SP 800-53 Configuration Management (CM) family are a good example of volatile controls. Information system configurations typically experience high rates of change. Unauthorized or unanalyzed changes in the system configuration often render the system vulnerable to exploits. Therefore, corresponding controls such as CM-6,

---

[33] Security control volatility is a measure of how frequently a control is likely to change over time subsequent to its implementation.

Configuration Settings, and CM-8, Information System Component Inventory, may require more frequent assessment and monitoring, preferably using automated, SCAP-validated tools that provide alerts and status on demand. Conversely, controls such as PS-2, Position Categorization, or PS-3, Personnel Screening, (from the NIST SP 800-53 Personnel Security family of controls) are not volatile in most organizational settings. They tend to remain static over long periods and would therefore typically require less frequent assessment.

- **System categorizations/impact levels**. In general, security controls implemented on systems that are categorized as high-impact are monitored more frequently than controls implemented on moderate-impact systems, which are in turn monitored more frequently than controls implemented on low-impact systems.[34]

- **Security controls or specific assessment objects providing critical functions**. Security controls or assessment objects that provide critical security functions (e.g., log management server, firewalls) are candidates for more frequent monitoring. Additionally, individual assessment objects that support critical security functions and/or are deemed critical to the system (in accordance with the Business Impact Analysis[35]) or to the organization may be candidates for more frequent monitoring.

- **Security controls with identified weaknesses.** Existing risks documented in security assessment reports (SARs) are considered for more frequent monitoring to ensure that risks stay within tolerance. Similarly, controls documented in the POA&M as having weaknesses are monitored more frequently until remediation of the weakness is complete. Note that not all weaknesses require the same level of monitoring. For example, weaknesses deemed in the SAR to be of minor or low-impact risk to the system or organization are monitored less frequently than a weakness with a higher-impact risk to the system or organization.

- **Organizational risk tolerance.**[36] Organizations with a low tolerance for risk (e.g., organizations that process, store, or transmit large amounts of proprietary and/or personally identifiable information (PII), organizations with numerous high-impact systems, organizations facing specific persistent threats) monitor more frequently than organizations with a higher tolerance for risk (e.g., organizations with primarily low- and moderate-impact systems that process, store, or transmit very little PII and/or proprietary information).

- **Threat information**. Organizations consider current credible threat information, including known exploits and attack patterns,[37] when establishing monitoring frequencies. For instance, if a specific attack is developed which exploits a vulnerability of an implemented technology, temporary or permanent increases to the monitoring frequencies for related controls or metrics may help provide protection from the threat.

- **Vulnerability information**.[38] Organizations consider current vulnerability information with respect to information technology products when establishing monitoring frequencies. For

---

[34] System impact levels are in accordance with FIPS 199 and NIST SP 800-60.

[35] See NIST SP 800-34, as amended, *Contingency Planning Guide for Federal Information Systems,* May 2010.

[36] See NIST SP 800-39, as amended, for more information on how to determine organizational risk tolerance.

[37] Attack patterns describe common methods for exploiting software, based on in-depth analysis of specific real-world attack examples. For more information, see the Common Attack Pattern Enumeration and Classification (CAPEC) site at http://capec.mitre.org/.

[38] For current vulnerability information, see http://www.kb.cert.org/vuls and http://nvd.nist.gov/.

instance, if a specific product manufacturer provides software patches monthly, an organization might consider conducting vulnerability scans on that product at least that often.

- **Risk assessment results**. Results from organizational and/or system-specific assessments of risk (either formal or informal) are examined and taken into consideration when establishing monitoring frequencies. For instance, if a system-specific risk assessment identifies potential threats and vulnerabilities related to nonlocal maintenance (NIST SP 800-53, MA-4), the organization considers more frequent monitoring of the records kept on nonlocal maintenance and diagnostic activities. If a risk scoring scheme is in place at the organization, the risk scores may be used as justification to increase or decrease the monitoring frequencies of related controls.

- **Output of monitoring strategy reviews**. Review and adjustment of the monitoring strategy is covered in detail in Section 3.6.

- **Reporting requirements**. Reporting requirements do not drive the ISCM strategy but may play a role in the frequency of monitoring. For instance, if OMB policy requires quarterly reports on the number of unauthorized components detected and corrective actions taken, the organization would monitor the system for unauthorized components at least quarterly.

Organizations focus on obtaining the data required at the determined frequencies and deploy their human and capitol resources accordingly. As automation capability or resources are added, organizations may consider increasing affected monitoring frequencies. Similarly, if resource availability decreases, the organization considers adjusting affected monitoring frequencies to ensure that security-related information is appropriately analyzed while continuing to meet organizational risk management requirements.

Many security controls in the NIST SP 800-53 catalog have multiple implementation requirements along with control enhancements that may also have multiple implementation requirements. It may be necessary to assess or monitor individual control requirements and/or control enhancements within a given control with differing frequencies. For instance, the control AC-2, Account Management, has ten separate requirements (a. through j.) within the base control and four control enhancements [(1) through (4)]. The monitoring frequency may vary for each requirement in accordance with the considerations discussed. For example, AC-2a involves the identification of account types. For a typical information system, once the account types have been identified and documented, they are not likely to change very often. For this reason, AC-2a is a candidate for relatively infrequent assessment. AC-2h involves the deactivation of temporary accounts and accounts of terminated or transferred users. Since personnel regularly come and go, a typical organization would most likely assess AC-2h on a more frequent basis than AC-2a. AC-2 (3) requires that the system automatically disable accounts after a specified time period of inactivity. As an automated control and one with typically high volatility, AC-2 (3) is a candidate for relatively frequent monitoring and also may serve to automate some of the base control requirements so that they can be monitored more frequently in accordance with the organizational ISCM strategy.

Organization and Mission/Business Processes Tiers.

At the mission/business processes tier, the organization establishes the minimum frequency with which each security control or metric is to be assessed or monitored. Frequencies are established across all organizational systems and common controls based on the criteria described above in this section. Common, hybrid, and system-specific security controls are addressed by organization and mission/business processes tier policy and procedures. Common controls are often inherited by a large number of organizational systems. The aggregate criticality of such controls may require more frequent assessments than would similar controls responsible for protecting a single system. Additionally, determining the frequency for assessing common controls includes the organization's determination of the trustworthiness of the common control provider. Common controls that are process-related (e.g., procedures/templates, PM controls) do not tend to be volatile and typically do not lend themselves well to automation. Still, the organization considers the volatility of such controls as well as related threat information when establishing assessment frequencies.

Primary Roles: Chief Information Officer, Senior Information Security Officer

Supporting Roles: Risk Executive (Function), Authorizing Officials, Common Control Provider, Information System Owner

Expected Input: Organizational risk assessment, organizational risk tolerance, current threat information, reporting requirements, current vulnerability information, output from monitoring strategy reviews

Expected Output: Organization-wide policies and procedures, recommended frequencies with which each security control and metric is assessed or monitored

Information Systems Tier.

At the information systems tier, system owners review the minimum monitoring/assessment frequencies established by organization and/or mission/business processes tier policy and determine if the minimum frequencies are adequate for a given information system. For some information systems, it may be necessary to assess specific controls or metrics with greater frequency than prescribed by the organization, again based on the criteria described above in this section. System owners also consider identification of specific system components that may require more frequent monitoring than other system components (e.g., public-facing servers, boundary protection devices, components deemed critical in the Business Impact Analysis).

Primary Roles: Information System Owner, Information System Security Officer

Supporting Roles: Authorizing Official, Senior Information Security Officer, Information Owner/Steward

Expected Input: Organizational strategy and procedures with minimum frequencies, current threat information, reporting requirements, current vulnerability information, output from monitoring strategy reviews, security assessment plans

Expected Output: Security assessment plans updated to reflect the frequency with which each system-specific security control is assessed and metrics are monitored

Event-Driven Assessments.

Events may occur that trigger the immediate need to assess security controls or verify security status outside of requirements expressed in the ISCM strategy. This may require an assessment that is unplanned, but of the type defined in the ISCM strategy or a customized assessment tailored to address an emerging need (e.g., a change in planned assessment or monitoring frequency). For example, if a Web application is added to a system, an existing ISCM process that includes configuration management and control, SIA, developmental vulnerability scans, etc., may be sufficient to assess controls implemented for the new Web application.

When defining criteria for event-driven assessments, organizations consider events such as incidents, new threat information, significant changes to systems and operating environments, new or additional mission responsibilities, and results of a security impact analysis (SIA) or assessment of risk.

Depending on the significance of the event, an event-driven assessment may trigger one or more system reauthorizations.

Primary Roles: Information System Owner/Common Control Provider, Authorizing Official, Information System Security Officer

Supporting Roles: Risk Executive (Function), Senior Information Security Officer, Security Control Assessor

Expected Input: Organizational risk assessment, organizational risk tolerance, current threat information, current vulnerability information, organizational priorities and expectations

Expected Output: Documented criteria and thresholds for event-driven assessments/authorizations (e.g., significant change procedures, policy and procedures on event-driven authorizations)

3.2.3 DEVELOP ISCM ARCHITECTURE

Organizations determine how the information will be collected and delivered within and between the tiers as well as external to the organization. The core requirements of an architecture implemented to support ISCM are data collection, data storage, data analysis capabilities, and retrieval and presentation (reporting) capabilities. Methodologies are standardized to facilitate efficiencies, intra- and inter-tier information exchange, correlation, and other analysis.

Organizations use automated tools, technologies, and methodologies where appropriate to allow for increased efficiencies and insight including those gained through collection, analysis and dissemination of large volumes of data from diverse sources. The architecture and associated policies and procedures are designed to minimize data calls and maximize data reuse.[39] Data feeds come from a heterogeneous mix of sources (e.g., authorization packages, training records, system logs) and accommodate different stakeholder views. Interoperable data specifications (e.g., SCAP, XML) enable data to be collected once and reused many times. Accountability for different facets of the security posture may reside with different roles or functions within an organization and hence require use of raw data in different metrics and contexts and at different

---

[39]   An example of an architecture for ISCM can be found in Draft NISTIR 7756, *CAESARS Framework Extension An Enterprise Continuous Monitoring Technical Reference Architecture (Draft)*.

intervals (e.g., security assessment and authorization, user awareness and training, and access control). Similarly, organizational missions and business functions have varied requirements for reporting and various drivers for action (e.g., changes to risk tolerance; changes in operational environments, including evolving threat activities; security architecture adjustments, security status reporting).

3.3 IMPLEMENT AN ISCM PROGRAM

ISCM is implemented in accordance with the strategy. Security-related information (data) is collected as required for predefined metrics, security control assessments are conducted, and the security-related information generated is reported in accordance with organizational policies and procedures. *All* security control classes (management, operational, and technical) and types (common, hybrid, and system-specific) are included in the organizational continuous monitoring program. Every control is monitored for effectiveness, and every control is subject to use in monitoring security status. Data sources include people, processes, technologies, the computing environment, as well as any existing relevant security control assessment reports.

Collection, analysis, and reporting of data are automated where possible. Whether manual or automated, the data collected is assembled for analysis and reported to the organizational officials charged with correlating and analyzing it in ways that are relevant for risk management activities. As indicated in the examples above, this may mean taking data from a variety of sources, collected at various points in time, and combining it in ways that are meaningful for the official receiving it at the time that it is requested. Part of the implementation stage of the continuous monitoring process is effectively organizing and delivering ISCM data to stakeholders in accordance with decision-making requirements. Tools and methodologies are chosen for the organization-wide ISCM architecture, in order to help ensure that risk-based decisions are informed by accurate, current security-related information.

Discrete security processes inform and are informed by ISCM data. Organizations also use ISCM data to inform processes that are not primarily used to control information security risk. Similarly, data from those processes can also be used to inform the ISCM program. Examples of processes that inform and are informed by ISCM include, but are not limited to, patch management, asset management, license management, configuration management, vulnerability management, and system authorization.

As described in Chapter Two, the ISCM data output from one process may serve as input to many others.

Primary Roles: Information System Owner, Common Control Provider, Information System Security Officer, Security Control Assessor

Supporting Roles: Risk Executive (Function), Authorizing Official, Chief Information Officer, Senior Information Security Officer

Expected Input: Organizational- and system-level policies and procedures on ISCM strategy, metrics, the Security Assessment Plan updated with assessment and monitoring frequencies, and automation specifications

Expected Outputs: Security-related information

3.4 ANALYZE DATA AND REPORT FINDINGS

Organizations develop procedures for analyzing and reporting assessment and monitoring results. This includes the specific staff/roles to receive ISCM reports, the content and format of the reports, the frequency of reports, and any tools to be used. Also included are requirements for analyzing and reporting results of controls that are not easily automated. It may be necessary to collect additional data to supplement or clarify security-related information under analysis or provided in initial reports. System- and mission/business-level staff receives and provides reports as required by organizational and mission/business-level policies and procedures.

3.4.1 ANALYZE DATA

Organizations analyze the security-related information resulting from ISCM. It may be necessary to collect additional data to supplement or clarify security-related information under analysis. The information to be analyzed is provided to organizational officials in a variety of ways, such as recurring reports, automated reports, ad hoc reports, data feeds, and database views.

Security-related information resulting from ISCM is analyzed in the context of stated risk tolerances, the potential impact that vulnerabilities may have on information systems, mission/business processes, and organization as a whole, and the potential impact of mitigation options. Even with real-time or near real-time organization-specific and system-specific security-related information, evolving vulnerability and threat data is always considered during the analysis. Organizational officials review the analyzed reports to determine whether to conduct mitigation activities or to transfer, avoid/reject, or accept risk. In some cases, authorizing officials may determine that accepting some specific risk is preferable to implementing a mitigating response. The rationale for such determinations may include organizational risk tolerance, negative impact to mission/business processes, or cost-effectiveness/return on investment of the implementation. Resolution of risk and the rationale for the decision is recorded in accordance with organizational policies and procedures.

Primary Roles: Risk Executive (Function), Chief Information Officer, Senior Information Security Officer; Authorization Officials, Security Control Assessors

Supporting Roles: Information System Owners, Common Control Providers, System Security Officers

Expected Input: Security-related information, organizational ISCM strategy, organizational risk tolerance, reporting requirements

Expected Output: Analysis of security status information for all tiers; updated System Security Plan, Security Assessment Report, and Plan of Action and Milestones; revised organizational risk management decisions

3.4.2 REPORT ON SECURITY CONTROL ASSESSMENTS

Organizations report on assessments of all implemented security controls for effectiveness in accordance with organizational requirements. Security-related information from assessments may be conveyed in templates or spreadsheets or collected and reported in an automated fashion. At the system level, security-related information from assessments directly supports ongoing authorization decisions and plans of action and milestones creation and tracking. Some security controls or elements of security controls, by definition, are security metrics (e.g., SI-4

Information System Monitoring). Hence, assessing the effectiveness of these controls results in monitoring the security status of the related metric.

Staff report assessment results in accordance with organizational policies and procedures. Reporting on additional metrics and/or assessment results may be required by higher-level organizations such as OMB. Organizations define security status reporting requirements in the ISCM strategy. This includes the specific staff/roles to receive ISCM reports, the content and format of the reports, the frequency of reports, and any tools to be used.

Tier 3 officials report on findings, document any system-level mitigations made, and/or provide recommendations to officials at Tiers 1 and 2. Organizational officials at Tiers 1 and 2 review Tier 3 findings to determine aggregate security status and the effectiveness and adequacy of *all controls* in meeting mission/business and organizational information security requirements. Information contained within a report will vary based on its recipient, frequency, purpose, supported tool sets, and metrics used. For example, the risk executive (function) may receive a general report on all systems annually and a detailed report on specific high-impact systems quarterly. The reports provided to the CIO and SISO may contain more granular technical data on all systems quarterly, and the AO may receive monthly comprehensive reports on the systems for which s/he is responsible. The computer incident response team (CIRT) lead may receive exception reports when alerts are generated, and network administrators may review dashboards showing network activity that is updated every minute, with summary metrics that are updated hourly or daily.[40] Organizations may consider more frequent reports for specific controls with more volatility or on controls for which there have been weaknesses or lack of compliance.

Organizations also define requirements for reporting results of controls, such as PM controls, that are not easily automated. Organizations develop procedures for collecting and reporting assessment and monitoring results, including results that are derived via manual methods, and for managing and collecting information from POA&Ms to be used for frequency determination, status reporting, and monitoring strategy revision.

Primary Roles: System Owner, Common Control Provider, System Security Officer, Security Control Assessor

Supporting Roles: Risk Executive (Function), Chief Information Officer, Chief Information Security Officer, Authorizing Official

Expected Input: Security-related information (assessment results); organizational ISCM policies and procedures; reporting requirements from the Authorizing Official, Chief Information Officer, Chief Information Security Officer, and/or Risk Executive (Function)

Expected Output: Reports on assessment results as required by organizational ISCM policies and procedures and by the Authorizing Official in support of ongoing authorization (or reauthorization)

3.4.3   REPORT ON SECURITY STATUS MONITORING

Organizations develop procedures for reporting on security status monitoring. Security status data is derived from monitoring the predefined metrics across the organization using output generated

---

[40]   Reporting frequencies noted here are for illustrative purposes only.

by organization-wide tools (often implemented as common controls). The organization-wide tools may be part of a specific system or systems, but the security-related information generated may not be system-specific.

Primary Roles: System Owner, Common Control Provider, System Security Officer, Security Control Assessor

Supporting Roles: Risk Executive (Function), Chief Information Officer, Chief Information Security Officer, Authorizing Official

Expected Input: Security-related information (security status data); organizational ISCM policies and procedures; reporting requirements from the Authorizing Official, Chief Information Officer, Chief Information Security Officer, and/or Risk Executive (Function)

Expected Output: Reports on security status as required by organizational ISCM policies and procedures and by the Authorizing Official in support of ongoing authorization (or re-authorization)

3.5 RESPOND TO FINDINGS

Security-related information obtained from monitoring is analyzed and met with appropriate responses. Response to findings at all tiers may include risk mitigation, risk acceptance, risk avoidance/rejection, or risk sharing/transfer, in accordance with organizational risk tolerance.[41]

Responses are coordinated with appropriate security management activities such as the security-focused configuration management program. At Tier 1, response to findings may result in changes to security policies around organizational governance. Tier 1's response may be constrained by the mission/business needs and the limitations of the enterprise architecture (including the human components), immutable governance policies, or other external drivers. At Tier 2, response to findings may include requests for additional security-related information, new or modified metrics, changes in mission/business processes, or Tier 3 reporting requirements, and/or additions or modifications to common control implementations. The Tier 2 response may be constrained by organizational governance policies and strategies as well as mission/business goals and objectives and limitations of organizational resources and infrastructure. At Tier 3, mitigation strategies have a direct and immediate impact on system-level risk and responses to findings may include implementation of additional controls, modifications to previously implemented controls, removal of systems' authorization to operate, changes to the frequency of monitoring, and/or additional or more detailed analysis of security-related information. System-level mitigations are made within constraints set by Tier 1 and 2 policies, requirements, and strategies, to ensure that organizational processes are not negatively affected.

Response strategies may be implemented over a period of time, documenting implementation plans in the system's Plan of Action and Milestones. As weaknesses are found, response actions are evaluated and any mitigation actions are conducted immediately or are added to the POA&M. Other key system documents are updated accordingly. Security controls that are modified, enhanced, or added as part of the response step of the continuous monitoring process are assessed

---

[41] For a detailed description of risk responses, see NIST SP 800-39, as amended.

to ensure that the new or revised controls are effective in their implementations.[42] Going forward, new or revised controls are included in the overall continuous monitoring strategy.

Primary Roles: System Owner, Common Control Provider, System Security Officer

Supporting Roles: Authorizing Official, Senior Information Security Officer, Information Owner/Steward

Expected Input: Reports on security status, reports on assessment results (e.g., Security Assessment Reports), organizational- and system-level risk assessments, Security Assessment Plans, System Security Plans, organizational procedures and templates

Expected Output: Decisions on risk responses, updated system security information (e.g., System Security Plans, POA&Ms, Security Assessment Reports), updated security status reports

3.6 REVIEW AND UPDATE THE MONITORING PROGRAM AND STRATEGY

ISCM strategies and programs are not static. Security control assessments, security status metrics, and monitoring and assessment frequencies change in accordance with the needs of the organization. The continuous monitoring strategy is reviewed to ensure that it sufficiently supports the organization in operating within acceptable risk tolerance levels, that metrics remain relevant, and that data is current and complete. The strategy review also identifies ways to improve organizational insight into security posture, effectively supports informed risk management decision making/ongoing authorizations, and improves the organization's ability to respond to known and emerging threats.

The organization establishes a procedure for reviewing and modifying all aspects of the ISCM strategy, including relevance of the overall strategy, accuracy in reflecting organizational risk tolerance, accuracy/correctness of measurements, and applicability of metrics, reporting requirements, and monitoring and assessment frequencies. If any of the data collected is not required for reporting purposes or found to be not useful in maintaining or improving the organization's security posture, then the organization considers saving resources by discontinuing that particular collection. Factors precipitating changes in the monitoring strategy may include, but are not limited to:

- Changes to core missions or business processes;

- Significant changes in the enterprise architecture (including addition or removal of systems);

- Changes in organizational risk tolerance;

- Changes in threat information;

- Changes in vulnerability information;

- Changes within information systems (including changes in categorization/impact level);

- Increase/decrease in POA&Ms related to specific controls;

---

[42] Changes to security controls are made after being fully tested, vetted, and reviewed in a test environment.

- Trend analyses of status reporting output;

- New federal laws or regulations; and/or

- Changes to reporting requirements.

Officials examine consolidated POA&M information to determine if there are common weaknesses/deficiencies among the organization's information systems and propose or request solutions. The aggregate POA&M information is used to allocate risk mitigation resources organization-wide and to make adjustments to the monitoring strategy. Similarly, status reports and metrics are analyzed to determine if there are any security trends that suggest changes to the monitoring strategy may be necessary. For instance, if weekly assessments of component inventories over a six-month period indicate that very few changes are being made in a given week and changes that *were* made are accurately reflected in the inventories, the organization may wish to reduce the frequency of monitoring component inventories to biweekly or monthly. Conversely, if biweekly audit record analyses over a six-month period indicate increases in anomalous events, the organization may wish to increase the frequency of audit record reviews to weekly.

An organization's ISCM strategy also changes as the organization's security program(s) and monitoring capabilities mature. In a fully mature program, security-related information collection and analysis are accomplished using standardized methods across the organization, as an integral part of mission and business processes, and automated to the fullest extent possible. In this case, the security program is mature enough to ensure that sufficient processes and procedures effectively secure the enterprise architecture in accordance with organizational risk tolerances, and to collect, correlate, analyze, and report on relevant security metrics.[43]

ISCM is a recursive process in the sense that the monitoring strategy is continually refined as the steps of the process repeat. Further, the organization-wide application of ISCM is accomplished through smaller or more narrowly focused instances of the similar efforts at the mission/business processes and systems tiers. In other words, the output of ISCM at Tier 3 is input to the implementation of the ISCM programs at Tiers 1 and 2. Working from the top of the pyramid in Figure 2-1 (Tier 1) to its bottom (Tier 3), upper-tier monitoring strategies set the parameters for lower-tier monitoring programs, and observations made at the lower tiers may result in changes to upper-tier monitoring strategies. The ISCM program itself must be monitored so that it can evolve with changes in organizational missions and objectives, operational environments, and threats.

Primary Roles: Senior Information Security Officer, Authorizing Official, Information System Owner/Common Control Provider

Supporting Roles: Risk Executive (Function), Chief Information Officer, Information System Security Officer

Expected Input: Trend analyses from existing monitoring; organizational risk tolerance information; information on new laws, regulations, reporting requirements; current threat and vulnerability information; other organizational information as required, updates to automation specifications

---

[43] See NIST SP 800-55, as amended, for more information on security metrics.

Expected Output: Revised ISCM strategy or a brief documented report noting review details and
that modifications to the strategy were not necessary (in accordance with the established review
process)

APPENDIX A

REFERENCES

LEGISLATION

1. E-Government Act [includes FISMA] (P.L. 107-347), December 2002.

POLICIES, DIRECTIVES, INSTRUCTIONS

1. Office of Management and Budget, Circular A-130, Appendix III, Transmittal Memorandum #4, *Management of Federal Information Resources*, November 2000.

2. Office of Management and Budget Memorandum M-02-01, *Guidance for Preparing and Submitting Security Plans of Action and Milestones*, October 2001.

3. Cyber Security Research and Development Act of 2002.

GUIDELINES

1. National Institute of Standards and Technology Special Publication 800-12, *An Introduction to Computer Security: The NIST Handbook*, October 1995.

2. National Institute of Standards and Technology Special Publication 800-34, Revision 1, *Contingency Planning Guide for Federal Information Systems,* May 2010.

3. National Institute of Standards and Technology Special Publication 800-37, Revision 1, *Guide for Applying the Risk Management Framework to Federal Information Systems: A Security Life Cycle Approach*, February 2010.

4. National Institute of Standards and Technology Special Publication 800-39, *Managing Information Security Risk: Organization, Mission, and Information System View,* March 2011.

5. National Institute of Standards and Technology Special Publication 800-40, Version 2, *Creating a Patch and Vulnerability Management Program*, November 2005.

6. National Institute of Standards and Technology Special Publication 800-53, Revision 3, *Recommended Security Controls for Federal Information Systems and Organizations*, August 2009.

7. National Institute of Standards and Technology Special Publication 800-53A, *Guide for Assessing the Security Controls in Federal Information Systems and Organizations: Building Effective Security Assessment Plans*, June 2010.

8. National Institute of Standards and Technology Special Publication 800-55, Revision 1, *Performance Measurement Guide for Information Security*, July 2008.

9. National Institute of Standards and Technology Special Publication 800-92, *Guide to Computer Log Management,* September 2006.

10. National Institute of Standards and Technology Special Publication 800-126, Revision 1, *The Technical Specification for the Security Content Automation Protocol (SCAP): SCAP Version 1.1,*February 2011.

11. National Institute of Standards and Technology Special Publication 800-128, *Guide for
    Security-Focused Configuration Management of Information Systems*, August 2011.

12. National Institute of Standards and Technology Interagency Report 7756, DRAFT,
    *CAESARS Framework Extension: an Enterprise Continuous Monitoring Technical
    Reference Architecture,* February 2011.

OTHER

1. Common Vulnerabilities and Exposures (CVE), http://cve.mitre.org/about/index.html.

2. Common Vulnerability Scoring System (CVSS), http://www.first.org/cvss/.

APPENDIX B

GLOSSARY

COMMON TERMS AND DEFINITIONS

This appendix provides definitions for security terminology used within Special Publication 800-137. The terms in the glossary are consistent with the terms used in the suite of FISMA-related security standards and guidelines developed by NIST. Unless otherwise stated, all terms used in this publication are also consistent with the definitions contained in the CNSS Instruction 4009, *National Information Assurance Glossary*.

Activities [NISTIR 7298]	An assessment object that includes specific protection-related pursuits or actions supporting an information system that involve people (e.g., conducting system backup operations, monitoring network traffic).
Adequate Security [OMB Circular A-130, Appendix III]	Security commensurate with the risk and the magnitude of harm resulting from the loss, misuse, or unauthorized access to or modification of information. This includes assuring that systems and applications used by the agency operate effectively and provide appropriate confidentiality, integrity, and availability, through the use of cost-effective management, personnel, operational, and technical controls.
Advanced Persistent Threats [NIST SP 800-39]	An adversary with sophisticated levels of expertise and significant resources, allowing it through the use of multiple different attack vectors (e.g., cyber, physical, and deception) to generate opportunities to achieve its objectives, which are typically to establish and extend footholds within the information technology infrastructure of organizations for purposes of continually exfiltrating information and/or to undermine or impede critical aspects of a mission, program, or organization, or place itself in a position to do so in the future; moreover, the advanced persistent threat pursues its objectives repeatedly over an extended period of time, adapting to a defender's efforts to resist it, and with determination to maintain the level of interaction needed to execute its objectives.
Agency	See *Executive Agency*.

Allocation [NISTIR 7298]	The process an organization employs to determine whether security controls are defined as system-specific, hybrid, or common.
	The process an organization employs to assign security controls to specific information system components responsible for providing a particular security capability (e.g., router, server, remote sensor).
Application [NISTIR 7298]	A software program hosted by an information system.
Assessment	See *Security Control Assessment*.
Assessment Findings [NISTIR 7298]	Assessment results produced by the application of an assessment procedure to a security control or control enhancement to achieve an assessment objective; the execution of a determination statement within an assessment procedure by an assessor that results in either a *satisfied* or *other than satisfied* condition.
Assessment Method [NISTIR 7298]	One of three types of actions (examine, interview, test) taken by assessors in obtaining evidence during an assessment.
Assessment Object [NISTIR 7298]	The item (specifications, mechanisms, activities, individuals) upon which an assessment method is applied during an assessment.
Assessment Objective [NISTIR 7298]	A set of determination statements that expresses the desired outcome for the assessment of a security control or control enhancement.
Assessment Procedure [NISTIR 7298]	A set of assessment *objectives* and an associated set of assessment *methods* and assessment *objects*.
Assessor	See *Security Control Assessor*.
Assurance [NISTIR 7298]	The grounds for confidence that the set of intended security controls in an information system are effective in their application.
Assurance Case [NISTIR 7298]	A structured set of arguments and a body of evidence showing that an information system satisfies specific claims with respect to a given quality attribute.
Authentication [FIPS 200]	Verifying the identity of a user, process, or device, often as a prerequisite to allowing access to resources in an information system.

Authenticity [CNSSI 4009]	The property of being genuine and being able to be verified and trusted; confidence in the validity of a transmission, a message, or message originator. See *Authentication*.
Authorization (to operate) [CNSSI 4009]	The official management decision given by a senior organizational official to authorize operation of an information system and to explicitly accept the risk to organizational operations (including mission, functions, image, or reputation), organizational assets, individuals, other organizations, and the Nation based on the implementation of an agreed-upon set of security controls.
Authorization Boundary [NIST SP 800-37]	All components of an information system to be authorized for operation by an authorizing official and excludes separately authorized systems, to which the information system is connected.
Authorizing Official (AO) [CNSSI 4009]	A senior (federal) official or executive with the authority to formally assume responsibility for operating an information system at an acceptable level of risk to organizational operations (including mission, functions, image, or reputation), organizational assets, individuals, other organizations, and the Nation.
Availability [44 U.S.C., Sec. 3542]	Ensuring timely and reliable access to and use of information.
Categorization	See *Security Categorization*.
Chief Information Officer (CIO) [PL 104-106, Sec. 5125(b)]	Agency official responsible for: 1) Providing advice and other assistance to the head of the executive agency and other senior management personnel of the agency to ensure that information technology is acquired and information resources are managed in a manner that is consistent with laws, Executive Orders, directives, policies, regulations, and priorities established by the head of the agency; 2) Developing, maintaining, and facilitating the implementation of a sound and integrated information technology architecture for the agency; and 3) Promoting the effective and efficient design and operation of all major information resources management processes for the agency, including improvements to work processes of the agency.
Chief Information Security Officer	See *Senior Agency Information Security Officer*.

Common Control [CNSSI 4009]	A security control that is inherited by one or more organizational information systems. See *Security Control Inheritance*.
Common Control Provider [NISTIR 7298]	An organizational official responsible for the development, implementation, assessment, and monitoring of common controls (i.e., security controls inherited by information systems).
Compensating Security Controls [NISTIR 7298]	The management, operational, and technical controls (i.e., safeguards or countermeasures) employed by an organization in lieu of the recommended controls in the low, moderate, or high baselines described in NIST Special Publication 800-53, that provide equivalent or comparable protection for an information system.
Comprehensive Testing [NISTIR 7298]	A test methodology that assumes explicit and substantial knowledge of the internal structure and implementation detail of the assessment object. Also known as white box testing.
Computer Incident Response Team (CIRT) [CNSSI 4009]	Group of individuals usually consisting of Security Analysts organized to develop, recommend, and coordinate immediate mitigation actions for containment, eradication, and recovery resulting from computer security incidents. Also called a Computer Security Incident Response Team (CSIRT) or a CIRC (Computer Incident Response Center, Computer Incident Response Capability, or Cyber Incident Response Team).
Confidentiality [44 U.S.C., Sec. 3542]	Preserving authorized restrictions on information access and disclosure, including means for protecting personal privacy and proprietary information.
Configuration Control (or Configuration Management) [CNSSI 4009]	Process for controlling modifications to hardware, firmware, software, and documentation to protect the information system against improper modifications before, during, and after system implementation.
Continuous Monitoring	Maintaining ongoing awareness to support organizational risk decisions. See *Information Security Continuous Monitoring, Risk Monitoring*, and *Status Monitoring*.
Controlled Interface [CNSSI 4009]	A boundary with a set of mechanisms that enforces the security policies and controls the flow of information between interconnected information systems.
Countermeasures [CNSSI 4009]	Actions, devices, procedures, techniques, or other measures that reduce the vulnerability of an information system. Synonymous with security controls and safeguards.

Coverage [NISTIR 7298]	An attribute associated with an assessment method that addresses the scope or breadth of the assessment objects included in the assessment (e.g., types of objects to be assessed and the number of objects to be assessed by type). The values for the coverage attribute, hierarchically from less coverage to more coverage, are basic, focused, and comprehensive.
Data Loss	The exposure of proprietary, sensitive, or classified information through either data theft or data leakage.
Depth [NISTIR 7298]	An attribute associated with an assessment method that addresses the rigor and level of detail associated with the application of the method. The values for the depth attribute, hierarchically from less depth to more depth, are basic, focused, and comprehensive.
Domain [CNSSI 4009]	An environment or context that includes a set of system resources and a set of system entities that have the right to access the resources as defined by a common security policy, security model, or security architecture. See *Security Domain*.
Environment of Operation [NISTIR 7298]	The physical surroundings in which an information system processes, stores, and transmits information.
Examine [NISTIR 7298]	A type of assessment method that is characterized by the process of checking, inspecting, reviewing, observing, studying, or analyzing one or more assessment objects to facilitate understanding, achieve clarification, or obtain evidence, the results of which are used to support the determination of security control effectiveness over time.
Executive Agency [41 U.S.C., Sec. 403]	An executive department specified in 5 U.S.C., Sec. 101; a military department specified in 5 U.S.C., Sec. 102; an independent establishment as defined in 5 U.S.C., Sec. 104(1); and a wholly owned Government corporation fully subject to the provisions of 31 U.S.C., Chapter 91.
Expected Output	Any data collected from monitoring and assessments as part of the ISCM strategy.
Federal Agency	See *Executive Agency*.
Federal Information System [40 U.S.C., Sec. 11331]	An information system used or operated by an executive agency, by a contractor of an executive agency, or by another organization on behalf of an executive agency.
High-Impact System [FIPS 200]	An information system in which at least one security objective (confidentiality, integrity, or availability) is assigned a FIPS 199 potential impact value of high.

Hybrid Security Control [CNSSI 4009]	A security control that is implemented in an information system in part as a common control and in part as a system-specific control. See *Common Control* and *System-Specific Security Control*.
Incident [FIPS 200]	An occurrence that actually or potentially jeopardizes the confidentiality, integrity, or availability of an information system or the information the system processes, stores, or transmits or that constitutes a violation or imminent threat of violation of security policies, security procedures, or acceptable use policies.
Individuals [NISTIR 7298]	An assessment object that includes people applying specifications, mechanisms, or activities.
Information [FIPS 199]	An instance of an information type.
Information Owner [CNSSI 4009]	Official with statutory or operational authority for specified information and responsibility for establishing the controls for its generation, collection, processing, dissemination, and disposal.
Information Resources [44 U.S.C., Sec. 3502]	Information and related resources, such as personnel, equipment, funds, and information technology.
Information Security [44 U.S.C., Sec. 3542]	The protection of information and information systems from unauthorized access, use, disclosure, disruption, modification, or destruction in order to provide confidentiality, integrity, and availability.
Information Security Architect [NISTIR 7298]	Individual, group, or organization responsible for ensuring that the information security requirements necessary to protect the organization's core missions and business processes are adequately addressed in all aspects of enterprise architecture including reference models, segment and solution architectures, and the resulting information systems supporting those missions and business processes.
Information Security Continuous Monitoring (ISCM)	Maintaining ongoing awareness of information security, vulnerabilities, and threats to support organizational risk management decisions. [Note: The terms "continuous" and "ongoing" in this context mean that security controls and organizational risks are assessed and analyzed at a frequency sufficient to support risk-based security decisions to adequately protect organization information.]

Information Security Continuous Monitoring (ISCM) Program	A program established to collect information in accordance with preestablished metrics, utilizing information readily available in part through implemented security controls.
Information Security Continuous Monitoring (ISCM) Process	A process to: • Define an ISCM strategy; • Establish an ISCM program; • Implement an ISCM program; • Analyze data and Report findings; • Respond to findings; and • Review and Update the ISCM strategy and program.
Information Security Program Plan [NISTIR 7298]	Formal document that provides an overview of the security requirements for an organization-wide information security program and describes the program management controls and common controls in place or planned for meeting those requirements.
Information Security Risk [NIST SP 800-39]	The risk to organizational operations (including mission, functions, image, reputation), organizational assets, individuals, other organizations, and the Nation due to the potential for unauthorized access, use, disclosure, disruption, modification, or destruction of information and /or information systems. See *Risk*.
Information System [44 U.S.C., Sec. 3502]	A discrete set of information resources organized for the collection, processing, maintenance, use, sharing, dissemination, or disposition of information.
Information System Boundary	See *Authorization Boundary*.
Information System Owner (or Program Manager) [NISTIR 7298]	Official responsible for the overall procurement, development, integration, modification, or operation and maintenance of an information system.
Information System Security Engineer [CNSSI 4009]	Individual assigned responsibility for conducting information system security engineering activities.
Information System Security Engineering [CNSSI 4009]	Process that captures and refines information security requirements and ensures that their integration into information technology component products and information systems through purposeful security design or configuration.

Information System-related Security Risks	Risks that arise through the loss of confidentiality, integrity, or availability of information or information systems and consider impacts to the organization (including assets, mission, functions, image, or reputation), individuals, other organizations, and the Nation. See *Risk*.
Information System Security Officer (ISSO) [CNSSI 4009]	Individual with assigned responsibility for maintaining the appropriate operational security posture for an information system or program.
Information Technology [40 U.S.C., Sec. 1401]	Any equipment or interconnected system or subsystem of equipment that is used in the automatic acquisition, storage, manipulation, management, movement, control, display, switching, interchange, transmission, or reception of data or information by the executive agency. For purposes of the preceding sentence, equipment is used by an executive agency if the equipment is used by the executive agency directly or is used by a contractor under a contract with the executive agency which: (i) requires the use of such equipment; or (ii) requires the use, to a significant extent, of such equipment in the performance of a service or the furnishing of a product. The term *information technology* includes computers, ancillary equipment, software, firmware, and similar procedures, services (including support services), and related resources.
Information Type [FIPS 199]	A specific category of information (e.g., privacy, medical, proprietary, financial, investigative, contractor sensitive, security management) defined by an organization or in some instances, by a specific law, Executive Order, directive, policy, or regulation.
Integrity [44 U.S.C., Sec. 3542]	Guarding against improper information modification or destruction, and includes ensuring information non-repudiation and authenticity.
Interview [NISTIR 7298]	A type of assessment method that is characterized by the process of conducting discussions with individuals or groups within an organization to facilitate understanding, achieve clarification, or lead to the location of evidence, the results of which are used to support the determination of security control effectiveness over time.
Intrusion Detection and Prevention System (IDPS) [NISTIR 7298]	Software that automates the process of monitoring the events occurring in a computer system or network and analyzing them for signs of possible incidents and attempting to stop detected possible incidents.

Malware [NISTIR 7298]	A program that is inserted into a system, usually covertly, with the intent of compromising the confidentiality, integrity, or availability of the victim's data, applications, or operating system or of otherwise annoying or disrupting the victim.
Management Controls [FIPS 200]	The security controls (i.e., safeguards or countermeasures) for an information system that focus on the management of risk and the management of information system security.
Mechanisms [NISTIR 7298]	An assessment object that includes specific protection-related items (e.g., hardware, software, or firmware) employed within or at the boundary of an information system.
Metrics [NISTIR 7298]	Tools designed to facilitate decision making and improve performance and accountability through collection, analysis, and reporting of relevant performance-related data.
National Security System [44 U.S.C., Sec. 3542]	Any information system (including any telecommunications system) used or operated by an agency or by a contractor of an agency, or other organization on behalf of an agency—(i) the function, operation, or use of which involves intelligence activities; involves cryptologic activities related to national security; involves command and control of military forces; involves equipment that is an integral part of a weapon or weapons system; or is critical to the direct fulfillment of military or intelligence missions (excluding a system that is to be used for routine administrative and business applications, for example, payroll, finance, logistics, and personnel management applications); or (ii) is protected at all times by procedures established for information that have been specifically authorized under criteria established by an Executive Order or an Act of Congress to be kept classified in the interest of national defense or foreign policy.
Operational Controls [FIPS 200]	The security controls (i.e., safeguards or countermeasures) for an information system that are primarily implemented and executed by people (as opposed to systems).
Organization [FIPS 200, Adapted]	An entity of any size, complexity, or positioning within an organizational structure (e.g., a federal agency, or, as appropriate, any of its operational elements).
Organizational Information Security Continuous Monitoring	Ongoing monitoring sufficient to ensure and assure effectiveness of security controls related to systems, networks, and cyberspace, by assessing security control implementation and organizational security status in accordance with organizational risk tolerance – and within a reporting structure designed to make real-time, data-driven risk management decisions.

Patch Management [CNSSI 4009]	The systematic notification, identification, deployment, installation, and verification of operating system and application software code revisions. These revisions are known as patches, hot fixes, and service packs.
Penetration Testing [NISTIR 7298]	A test methodology in which assessors, using all available documentation (e.g., system design, source code, manuals) and working under specific constraints, attempt to circumvent the security features of an information system.
Plan of Action & Milestones (POA&M) [OMB Memorandum 02-01]	A document that identifies tasks needing to be accomplished. It details resources required to accomplish the elements of the plan, any milestones in meeting the tasks, and scheduled completion dates for the milestones.
Potential Impact [FIPS 199]	The loss of confidentiality, integrity, or availability could be expected to have: (i) a *limited* adverse effect (FIPS 199 low); (ii) a *serious* adverse effect (FIPS 199 moderate); or (iii) a *severe* or *catastrophic* adverse effect (FIPS 199 high) on organizational operations, organizational assets, or individuals.
Records [CNSSI 4009]	The recordings (automated and/or manual) of evidence of activities performed or results achieved (e.g., forms, reports, test results), which serve as a basis for verifying that the organization and the information system are performing as intended. Also used to refer to units of related data fields (i.e., groups of data fields that can be accessed by a program and that contain the complete set of information on particular items).
Resilience [NIST SP 800-39, Adapted]	The ability to continue to: (i) operate under adverse conditions or stress, even if in a degraded or debilitated state, while maintaining essential operational capabilities; and (ii) recover to an effective operational posture in a time frame consistent with mission needs.
Risk [FIPS 200, Adapted]	A measure of the extent to which an entity is threatened by a potential circumstance or event, and typically a function of: (i) the adverse impacts that would arise if the circumstance or event occurs; and (ii) the likelihood of occurrence. [Note: Information system-related security risks are those risks that arise from the loss of confidentiality, integrity, or availability of information or information systems and reflect the potential adverse impacts to organizational operations (including mission, functions, image, or reputation), organizational assets, individuals, other organizations, and the Nation. Adverse impacts to the Nation include, for example, compromises to information systems that support critical infrastructure applications or are paramount to government continuity of operations as defined by the Department of Homeland Security.]

Risk Assessment [CNSSI 4009]	The process of identifying risks to organizational operations (including mission, functions, image, reputation), organizational assets, individuals, other organizations, and the Nation, resulting from the operation of an information system. Part of risk management, incorporates threat and vulnerability analyses, and considers mitigations provided by security controls planned or in place. Synonymous with risk analysis.
Risk Executive (Function) [CNSSI 4009]	An individual or group within an organization that helps to ensure that: (i) security risk-related considerations for individual information systems, to include the authorization decisions, are viewed from an organization-wide perspective with regard to the overall strategic goals and objectives of the organization in carrying out its missions and business functions; and (ii) managing information system-related security risks is consistent across the organization, reflects organizational risk tolerance, and is considered along with organizational risks affecting mission/business success.
Risk Management [FIPS 200, Adapted]	The program and supporting processes to manage information security risk to organizational operations (including mission, functions, image, reputation), organizational assets, individuals, other organizations, and the Nation, and includes: (i) establishing the context for risk-related activities; (ii) assessing risk; (iii) responding to risk once determined; and (iv) monitoring risk over time.
Risk Monitoring	Maintaining ongoing awareness of an organization's risk environment, risk management program, and associated activities to support risk decisions.
Risk Response [NIST SP 800-39]	Accepting, avoiding, mitigating, sharing, or transferring risk to organizational operations (mission, functions, image, or reputation), organizational assets, individuals, other organizations, and the Nation.
Risk Tolerance [NISTIR 7298]	The level of risk an entity is willing to assume in order to achieve a potential desired result.
Safeguards [CNSSI 4009]	Protective measures prescribed to meet the security requirements (i.e., confidentiality, integrity, and availability) specified for an information system. Safeguards may include security features, management constraints, personnel security, and security of physical structures, areas, and devices. Synonymous with security controls and countermeasures.
Security Authorization	See *Authorization*.

Security Automation Domain	An information security area that includes a grouping of tools, technologies, and data.
Security Categorization [CNSSI 1253, FIPS 199]	The process of determining the security category for information or an information system. Security categorization methodologies are described in CNSS Instruction 1253 for national security systems and in FIPS 199 for other than national security systems.
Security Control Assessment [CNSSI 4009, Adapted]	The testing and/or evaluation of the management, operational, and technical security controls in an information system to determine the extent to which the controls are implemented correctly, operating as intended, and producing the desired outcome with respect to meeting the security requirements for the system.
Security Control Assessor [NISTIR 7298]	The individual, group, or organization responsible for conducting a security control assessment.
Security Control Baseline [FIPS 200, Adapted]	One of the sets of minimum security controls defined for federal information systems in NIST Special Publication 800-53 and CNSS Instruction 1253.
Security Control Effectiveness	The measure of correctness of implementation (i.e., how consistently the control implementation complies with the security plan) and how well the security plan meets organizational needs in accordance with current risk tolerance.
Security Control Inheritance [CNSSI 4009]	A situation in which an information system or application receives protection from security controls (or portions of security controls) that are developed, implemented, assessed, authorized, and monitored by entities other than those responsible for the system or application; entities either internal or external to the organization where the system or application resides. See *Common Control*.
Security Controls [FIPS 199]	The management, operational, and technical controls (i.e., safeguards or countermeasures) prescribed for an information system to protect the confidentiality, integrity, and availability of the system and its information.
Security Domain [CNSSI 4009]	A domain that implements a security policy and is administered by a single authority.
Security Impact Analysis [NIST SP 800-53]	The analysis conducted by an organizational official to determine the extent to which changes to the information system have affected the security state of the system.
Security Incident	See *Incident*.

Security Management Dashboard [NIST SP 800-128]	A tool that consolidates and communicates information relevant to the organizational security posture in near real-time to security management stakeholders.
Security Objective [FIPS 199]	Confidentiality, integrity, or availability.
Security Plan [NISTIR 7298]	Formal document that provides an overview of the security requirements for an information system or an information security program and describes the security controls in place or planned for meeting those requirements. See *System Security Plan* or *Information Security Program Plan*.
Security Policy [CNSSI 4009]	A set of criteria for the provision of security services.
Security Posture [CNSSI 4009]	The security status of an organization's networks, information, and systems based on IA resources (e.g., people, hardware, software, policies) and capabilities in place to manage the defense of the organization and to react as the situation changes.
Security Requirements [FIPS 200]	Requirements levied on an information system that are derived from applicable laws, Executive Orders, directives, policies, standards, instructions, regulations, procedures, or organizational mission/business case needs to ensure the confidentiality, integrity, and availability of the information being processed, stored, or transmitted.
Security Status	See *Security Posture*.
Senior (Agency) Information Security Officer (SISO) [44 U.S.C., Sec. 3544]	Official responsible for carrying out the Chief Information Officer responsibilities under the Federal Information Security Management Act (FISMA) and serving as the Chief Information Officer's primary liaison to the agency's authorizing officials, information system owners, and information system security officers. [Note: Organizations subordinate to federal agencies may use the term *Senior Information Security Officer* or *Chief Information Security Officer* to denote individuals filling positions with similar responsibilities to Senior Agency Information Security Officers.]
Senior Information Security Officer	See *Senior Agency Information Security Officer*.

Specification [NISTIR 7298]	An assessment object that includes document-based artifacts (e.g., policies, procedures, plans, system security requirements, functional specifications, and architectural designs) associated with an information system.
Status Monitoring	Monitoring the information security metrics defined by the organization in the information security ISCM strategy.
Subsystem [NISTIR 7298]	A major subdivision of an information system consisting of information, information technology, and personnel that performs one or more specific functions.
System	See *Information System*.
System Development Life Cycle (SDLC) [CNSSI 4009]	The scope of activities associated with a system, encompassing the system's initiation, development and acquisition, implementation, operation and maintenance, and ultimately its disposal.
System Development Life Cycle (SDLC) [CNSSI 4009, Adapted]	The scope of activities associated with a system, encompassing the system's initiation, development and acquisition, implementation, operation and maintenance, and ultimately its disposal that instigates another system initiation.
System Security Plan [FIPS 200]	Formal document that provides an overview of the security requirements for an information system and describes the security controls in place or planned for meeting those requirements.
System-Specific Security Control [CNSSI 4009]	A security control for an information system that has not been designated as a common security control or the portion of a hybrid control that is to be implemented within an information system.
Tailoring [CNSSI 4009]	The process by which a security control baseline is modified based on: (i) the application of scoping guidance; (ii) the specification of compensating security controls, if needed; and (iii) the specification of organization-defined parameters in the security controls via explicit assignment and selection statements.
Technical Controls [FIPS 200]	The security controls (i.e., safeguards or countermeasures) for an information system that are primarily implemented and executed by the information system through mechanisms contained in the hardware, software, or firmware components of the system.
Test [NISTIR 7298]	A type of assessment method that is characterized by the process of exercising one or more assessment objects under specified conditions to compare actual with expected behavior, the results of which are used to support the determination of security control effectiveness over time.

Threat [CNSSI 4009, Adapted]	Any circumstance or event with the potential to adversely impact organizational operations (including mission, functions, image, or reputation), organizational assets, individuals, other organizations, or the Nation through an information system via unauthorized access, destruction, disclosure, modification of information, and/or denial of service.
Threat Information [CNSSI 4009, Adapted]	Analytical insights into trends, technologies, or tactics of an adversarial nature affecting information systems security.
Threat Source [FIPS 200]	The intent and method targeted at the intentional exploitation of a vulnerability or a situation and method that may accidentally trigger a vulnerability. Synonymous with threat agent.
Vulnerability [CNSSI 4009]	Weakness in an information system, system security procedures, internal controls, or implementation that could be exploited or triggered by a threat source.
Vulnerability Assessment [CNSSI 4009]	Formal description and evaluation of the vulnerabilities in an information system.
White Box Testing	See *Comprehensive Testing*.

APPENDIX C

ACRONYMS

COMMON ABBREVIATIONS

AO	Authorizing Official
CAPEC	Common Attack Pattern Enumeration & Classification
CIO	Chief Information Officer
CIRT	Computer Incident Response Team
COTS	Commercial Off-The-Shelf
CVSS	Common Vulnerability Scoring System
CVE	Common Vulnerabilities and Exposures
CWE	Common Weakness Enumeration
CWSS	Common Weakness Scoring System
DLP	Data Loss Prevention
FDCC	Federal Desktop Core Configuration
FISMA	Federal Information Security Management Act of 2002
IDPS	Intrusion Detection and Prevention System
ISCM	Information Security Continuous Monitoring
ISO	Information System Owner
ISSO	Information System Security Officer
IT	Information Technology
NCP	National Checklist Program
NVD	National Vulnerability Database
OCIL	Open Checklist Interactive Language
OMB	Office of Management and Budget
OVAL	Open Vulnerability and Assessment Language
PII	Personally Identifiable Information
PM	Program Management
POA&M	Plan Of Action & Milestones
RMF	Risk Management Framework
SAR	Security Assessment Report
SCAP	Security Content Automation Protocol
SDLC	System Development Life Cycle

SIA	Security Impact Analysis
SIEM	Security Information and Event Management
SISO	Senior Information Security Officer
SP	Special Publication
SwAAP	Software Assurance Automation Protocol
USGCB	United States Government Configuration Baseline
XCCDF	eXtensible Configuration Checklist Description Format
XML	Extensible Markup Language

APPENDIX D

TECHNOLOGIES FOR ENABLING ISCM

O rganizations can make more effective use of their security budgets by implementing
technologies to automate many of the ISCM activities in support of organizational risk
management policy and strategy, operational security, internal and external compliance,
reporting, and documentation needs. Organizations may choose to follow a reference architecture,
such as NIST CAESARS Framework Extension, to implement ISCM technologies.[44] There are a
variety of tools and technologies available that an organization can use to efficiently and
effectively gather, aggregate, analyze, and report data ranging from continuously monitoring the
security status of its enterprise architecture and operating environment(s) down to components of
individual information systems. These tools and technologies can enable and assist automated
monitoring in support of a variety of organizational processes including but not limited to:

- Ongoing assessments of security control effectiveness;

- Reporting of security status at the appropriate level of granularity to personnel with security
  responsibilities;

- Management of risk and verification and assessment of mitigation activities;

- Assurance of compliance with high-level internal and external requirements; and

- Analysis of the security impact of changes to the operational environment.

The tools and technologies discussed in this appendix leverage the strategies, policies, and roles
and responsibilities of the overall ISCM program, and can assist organizations in their efforts to
automate the implementation, assessment, and monitoring of many NIST SP 800-53 security
controls. Though these tools and technologies lend themselves primarily to the continuous
monitoring of technical security controls that can be automated, they can provide evidence, in an
automated manner, to support the existence and effectiveness of nontechnical security controls or
parts of technical security controls that cannot be easily automated. Automation is achieved
through a variety of commercial off-the-shelf (COTS) and government off-the-shelf (GOTS)
products, built-in operating system capabilities, and custom tools and scripting that use
standardized automation specifications.

It is important to understand and appreciate the need to assess the effectiveness of all security
controls, particularly nontechnical security controls, periodically. Data collected from automated
tools may not provide feedback on the existence and the effectiveness of nontechnical security
controls. It may be possible in some cases to make certain inferences about the effectiveness of
nontechnical security controls based on data collected from automated tools. While it may not be
possible to use automated tools and technologies to monitor adherence to policies and procedures,
it may be possible to monitor associated security objectives in an automated fashion.

---

[44]   For more information, please refer to DRAFT NISTIR 7756, as amended, *CAESARS Framework Extension An
Enterprise Continuous Monitoring Technical Reference Architecture.*

The Open Checklist Interactive Language (OCIL), discussed in Section D.3.1, may be used to partially automate certain controls that require human interaction and can be verified in a question and answer type format. For example, it may be possible to create an automated questionnaire to gather information related to annual security awareness training.

The validity of the security-related information collected continuously or on demand from automated tools assumes the continued effectiveness of the underlying management and operational security controls. As such, the value of automated tools and technologies, including those that perform direct data gathering and aggregation and analysis of data, is dependent upon the operational processes supporting their use. For organizations to realize the operational security benefits and for the tools and technologies to provide an accurate security status, knowledgeable staff should select, implement, operate, and maintain these tools and technologies, as well as all underlying security controls, interpret the monitoring data obtained, and select and implement appropriate remediation.

This appendix discusses the role of tools and technologies in automating many ISCM activities. It discusses common tools, technologies, and open specifications used to collect, analyze, and meaningfully represent data in support of continuous monitoring of an organization's security posture, including providing visibility into the information assets, awareness of threats and vulnerabilities, and status of security control effectiveness. Examples of security controls that can be automated using the various technologies are included. This is not an exhaustive set of examples. New products and technologies continue to reach the market. Controls commonly automated but that do not appear as examples associated with the technologies named below include those where automation is achieved through capabilities built into operating systems, custom tools and scripts, or a combination of several tools and capabilities.[45]

D.1 TECHNOLOGIES FOR DATA GATHERING

Data gathering technologies are those that provide the capability to observe, detect, prevent, or log known security threats and vulnerabilities, and/or remediate or manage various aspects of security controls implemented to address those threats and vulnerabilities. These technologies are primarily implemented at the information systems level (Tier 3). However, they can be configured to support an organization's ongoing security monitoring needs up through mission/business processes and information security governance metrics. Implementing a tool across an organization allows systems within that organization to inherit and leverage said capability.

A security automation domain is an information security area that includes a grouping of tools, technologies, and data. Data within the domains is captured, correlated, analyzed, and reported to present the security status of the organization that is represented by the domains monitored. Security automation provides standardized specifications that enable the interoperability and flow of data between these domains. Monitoring capabilities are achieved through the use of a variety of tools and techniques. The granularity of the information collected is determined by the organization, based on its monitoring objectives and the capability of the enterprise architecture to support such activities.

---

[45] Examples of such controls that lend themselves to full or partial automation through security engineering or the use of proprietary/third party software and log management tools include account management, security training records, incident reporting, and physical access control.

This section describes the tools and technologies within eleven security automation domains that support continuous monitoring:

- Vulnerability Management;

- Patch Management;

- Event Management;

- Incident Management;

- Malware Detection;

- Asset Management;

- Configuration Management;

- Network Management;

- License Management;

- Information Management; and

- Software Assurance.

The domains are pictured in Figure D-1.

Figure D-1. Security Automation Domains

D.1.1 VULNERABILITY AND PATCH MANAGEMENT

A vulnerability is a software flaw that introduces a potential security exposure. The number of vulnerabilities discovered and patches developed to address those vulnerabilities continues to grow, making manual patching of systems and system components an increasingly difficult task. To the extent possible, organizations should identify, report, and remediate vulnerabilities in a coordinated, organization-wide manner using automated vulnerability and patch management tools and technologies.

Vulnerability scanners are commonly used in organizations to identify known vulnerabilities on hosts and networks and on commonly used operating systems and applications. These scanning tools can proactively identify vulnerabilities, provide a fast and easy way to measure exposure, identify out-of-date software versions, validate compliance with an organizational security policy, and generate alerts and reports about identified vulnerabilities.

Patch management tools scan for vulnerabilities on systems and system components participating in an organization's patching solution, provide information regarding needed patches and other software updates on affected devices, and allow an administrator to decide on the patching implementation process. Patch management tools and utilities are available from various vendors to assist in the automated identification, distribution, and reporting of software patches. It is critical to understand the impact of patches before applying and to deploy them within the context of a defined patch management policy, providing assurance that systems will not lose critical functionality due to an unintended side effect of a patch. In some cases where a patch cannot be deployed, other compensating security controls may be necessary.

The implementation and effective use of vulnerability assessment and patch management technologies[46] can assist organizations in automating the implementation, assessment, and

---

[46]   For more information, please refer to NIST SP 800-40, as amended, *Creating a Patch and Vulnerability*

continuous monitoring of several NIST SP 800-53 security controls including SI-2, Flaw Remediation; CA-2, Security Assessments; CA-7, Continuous Monitoring; CM-3, Configuration Change Control; IR-4, Incident Handling; IR-5, Incident Monitoring; MA-2, Controlled Maintenance; RA-5, Vulnerability Scanning; SA-11, Developer Security Testing; and SI-11, Error Handling. Vulnerability assessment and patch management technologies may also provide supporting data to assist organizations in responding to higher-level reporting requirements in the areas of configuration and vulnerability management.

D.1.2 EVENT AND INCIDENT MANAGEMENT

Event management involves monitoring and responding to as necessary, observable occurrences in a network or system. A variety of tools and technologies exist to monitor events, such as intrusion detection systems and logging mechanisms. Some tools may detect events based on known attack signatures, while others detect anomalies in behavior or performance that could indicate an attack. Certain events may signal that an incident has occurred, which is a violation or imminent threat of violation of computer security policies, acceptable use policies, or standard computer security practices. Incident management tools may assist in detecting, responding to, and limiting the consequences of a malicious cyber attack against an organization.

A log is a record of the events occurring within an organization's systems and networks. Logs are composed of log entries; each entry contains information related to a specific event that has occurred within a system or system component. Many logs within an organization contain records related to computer security. These computer security logs can be generated by many sources, including security software such as malware protection software, firewalls, and intrusion detection and prevention systems, operating systems on servers, workstations, networking equipment, and applications.[47]

The number, volume, and variety of security logs have increased greatly, which has created the need for information system security log management – the process of generating, transmitting, storing, analyzing, and disposing of security log data. Log management is essential for ensuring that security records are stored in sufficient detail for an appropriate period of time. Logs are a key resource when performing auditing and forensic analysis, supporting internal investigations, establishing baselines, and identifying operational trends and long-term problems. Routine log analysis is beneficial for identifying security incidents, policy violations, fraudulent activity, and operational problems, and as such, supports an ISCM capability.

The implementation and effective use of logging and log management tools and technologies can assist organizations in automating the implementation, assessment, and continuous monitoring of several NIST SP 800-53 security controls including AU-2, Auditable Events; AU-3, Content of Audit Records; AU-4, Audit Storage Capacity; AU-5, Response to Audit Processing Failures; AU-6, Audit Review, Analysis, and Reporting; AU-7, Audit Reduction and Report Generation; AU-8, Time Stamps; AU-12, Audit Generation; CA-2, Security Assessments; CA-7, Continuous Monitoring; IR-5, Incident Monitoring; RA-3, Risk Assessment; and SI-4, Information system Monitoring.

Intrusion detection is the process of monitoring the events occurring in a computer system or network and analyzing them for signs of possible incidents, which are violations or imminent

---

Management Program.

[47] For more information, please refer to NIST SP 800-92, *Guide to Computer Security Log Management.*

threats of violation of computer security policies, acceptable use policies, or standard security practices. *Intrusion prevention* is the process of performing intrusion detection and attempting to stop possible incidents as they are detected. Intrusion detection and prevention systems (IDPSs)[48] are focused primarily on identifying possible incidents, logging information about them, attempting to stop them, and reporting them to security administrators for further analysis and action.

IDPSs typically are used to record information related to observed events, notify security administrators of important observed events, and automatically generate reports, with remediation actions performed manually after human review of the report. Many IDPSs can also be configured to respond to a detected threat using a variety of techniques, including changing security configurations or blocking the attack.

Within the context of an ISCM program, IDPSs can be used to supply evidence of the effectiveness of security controls (e.g., policies, procedures, and other implemented technical controls), document existing threats, and deter unauthorized use of information systems. The implementation and effective use of IDPSs can also assist organizations in automating the implementation, assessment, and continuous monitoring of several NIST SP 800-53 security controls including AC-4, Information Flow Enforcement; AC-17, Remote Access; AC-18, Wireless Access; AU-2, Auditable Events; AU-6, Audit Review, Analysis, and Reporting; AU-12, Audit Generation; AU-13, Monitoring for Information Disclosure; CA-2, Security Assessments; CA-7, Continuous Monitoring; IR-5, Incident Monitoring; RA-3, Risk Assessment; SC-7, Boundary Protection; SI-3, Malicious Code Protection; SI-4, Information System Monitoring; and SI-7, Software and Information Integrity. IDPSs may also provide supporting data to assist organizations in meeting US-CERT incident reporting requirements and in responding to OMB and agency CIO reporting requirements in the areas of system and connections inventory, security incident management, boundary protections, and configuration management.

D.1.3 MALWARE DETECTION

Malware detection[49] provides the ability to identify and report on the presence of viruses, Trojan horses, spyware, or other malicious code on or destined for a target system. Organizations typically employ malware detection mechanisms at information system entry and exit points (e.g., firewalls, email servers, Web servers, proxy servers, remote access servers) and at endpoint devices (e.g., workstations, servers, mobile computing devices) on the network to detect and remove malicious code transported by electronic mail, electronic mail attachments, Web accesses, removable media or other means, or inserted through the exploitation of information system vulnerabilities.

Malware detection mechanisms can be configured to perform periodic scans of information systems, as well as real-time scans of files from external sources as the files are downloaded, opened, or executed in accordance with organizational security policy. Malware detection mechanisms can frequently take a predetermined action in response to malicious code detection.

---

[48] For more information, please refer to NIST SP 800-94, as amended, *Guide to Intrusion Detection and Prevention Systems (IDPS)*.

[49] For more information, please refer to NIST SP 800-83, as amended, *Guide to Malware Incident Prevention and Handling*.

In addition to malware detection, a variety of technologies and methods exist to limit or eliminate the effects of malicious code attacks. Used in conjunction with configuration management and control procedures and strong software integrity controls, malware detection mechanisms can be even more effective in preventing execution of unauthorized code. Additional risk mitigation measures, such as secure coding practices, trusted procurement processes, and regular monitoring of secure configurations, can help to ensure that unauthorized functions are not performed.

The implementation and effective use of malware detection technologies can assist organizations in automating the implementation, assessment, and continuous monitoring of several NIST SP 800-53 security controls, including CA-2, Security Assessments; CA-7, Continuous Monitoring; IR-5, Incident Monitoring; RA-3, Risk Assessment; SA-12, Supply Chain Protection; SA-13, Trustworthiness; SI-3, Malicious Code Protection; SI-4, Information System Monitoring; SI-7, Software and Information Integrity; and SI-8, Spam Protection. Malware detection technologies may also provide supporting data to assist organizations in meeting US-CERT incident reporting requirements and in responding to OMB and agency CIO reporting requirements related to incident management, remote access, and boundary protections.

D.1.4 ASSET MANAGEMENT

Asset management tools help maintain inventory of software and hardware within the organization. This can be accomplished via a combination of system configuration, network management, and license management tools, or with a special-purpose tool. Asset management software tracks the life cycle of an organization's assets and provides tools such as remote management of assets and various automated management functions.

The implementation and effective use of asset management technologies can assist organizations in automating the implementation, assessment, and continuous monitoring of several NIST SP 800-53 security controls including CA-7, Continuous Monitoring; CM-2, Baseline Configuration; CM-3, Configuration Change Control; CM-4, Security Impact Analysis; CM-8, Information System Component Inventory; and SA-10, Developer Configuration Management.

D.1.5 CONFIGURATION MANAGEMENT

Configuration management tools allow administrators to configure settings, monitor changes to settings, collect setting status, and restore settings as needed. Managing the numerous configurations found within information systems and network components has become almost impossible using manual methods. Automated solutions may lower the cost of configuration management efforts while enhancing efficiency and improving reliability.

System configuration scanning tools provide the automated capability to audit and assess a target system to determine its compliance with a defined secure baseline configuration. A user may confirm compliance with, and identify deviations from, checklists appropriate for relevant operating systems and/or applications.

If an information system or system component is unknowingly out of synchronization with the approved secure configurations as defined by the organization's baseline configurations and the System Security Plan, organization officials and system owners may have a false sense of security. An opportunity to take actions that would otherwise limit vulnerabilities and help protect the organization from attack would subsequently be missed. Monitoring activities offer the organization better visibility into the state of security for its information systems, as defined by the security metrics being monitored.

Identity and account configuration management tools allow an organization to manage identification credentials, access control, authorization, and privileges. Identity management systems may also enable and monitor physical access control based on identification credentials. Identity and account configuration management tools often have the ability to automate tasks such as account password resets and other account maintenance activities. These systems also monitor and report on activities such as unsuccessful login attempts, account lockouts, and resource access.

There are a wide variety of configuration management tools available to support an organization's needs. When selecting a configuration management tool, organizations should consider tools that can pull information from a variety of sources and components. Organizations should choose tools that are based on open specifications such as SCAP; that support organization-wide interoperability, assessment, and reporting; that provide the ability to tailor and customize output; and that allow for data consolidation into SIEM tools and management dashboards.

The implementation and effective use of configuration management technologies can assist organizations in automating the implementation, assessment, and continuous monitoring of several NIST SP 800-53 security controls including AC-2, Account Management; AC-3, Access Enforcement; AC-5, Separation of Duties; AC-7, Unsuccessful Login Attempts; AC-9, Previous Logon (Access) Notification; AC-10, Concurrent Session Control; AC-11, Session Lock; AC-19, Access Control for Mobile Devices; AC-20, Use of External Information Systems; AC-22, Publicly Accessible Content; CA-2, Security Assessments; CA-7, Continuous Monitoring; CM-2, Baseline Configuration; CM-3, Configuration Change Control; CM-5, Access Restrictions for Change; CM-6, Configuration Settings; CM-7, Least Functionality; IA-2, Identification and Authentication (Organizational Users); IA-3, Device Identification and Authentication; IA-4, Identifier Management; IA-5, Authenticator Management; IA-8, Identification and Authentication (Non-Organizational Users); IR-5, Incident Monitoring; MA-5, Maintenance Personnel; PE-3, Physical Access Control; RA-3, Risk Assessment; SA-7, User Installed Software; SA-10, Developer Configuration Management; and SI-2, Flaw Remediation. Organization-wide security configuration management and engineering technologies may also provide supporting data to assist organizations in responding to higher-level compliance reporting requirements in the areas of configuration and asset management.

D.1.6 NETWORK MANAGEMENT

Network configuration management tools include host discovery, inventory, change control, performance monitoring, and other network device management capabilities. Some network configuration management tools automate device configuration and validate device compliance against pre-configured policies. Network management tools may be able to discover unauthorized hardware and software on the network, such as a rogue wireless access point.

The implementation and effective use of network management technologies can assist organizations in automating the implementation, assessment, and continuous monitoring of several NIST SP 800-53 security controls including AC-4, Information Flow Enforcement; AC-17, Remote Access; AC-18, Wireless Access; CA-7, Continuous Monitoring; CM-2, Baseline Configuration; CM-3, Configuration Change Control; CM-4, Security Impact Analysis; CM-6, Configuration Settings; CM-8, Information System Component Inventory; SC-2, Application Partitioning; SC-5, Denial of Service Protection; SC-7, Boundary Protection; SC-10, Network Disconnect; SC-32, Information System Partitioning; and SI-4, Information System Monitoring.

D.1.7 LICENSE MANAGEMENT

Similar to systems and network devices, software and applications are also a relevant data source for ISCM. Software asset and licensing information may be centrally managed by a software asset management tool to track license compliance, monitor usage status, and manage the software asset life cycle. License management tools offer a variety of features to automate inventory, utilization monitoring and restrictions, deployment, and patches for software and applications.

The implementation and effective use of license management technologies can assist organizations in automating the implementation, assessment, and continuous monitoring of several NIST SP 800-53 security controls including CA-7, Continuous Monitoring; CM-8, Information System Component Inventory; and SA-6, Software Usage Restrictions.

D.1.8 INFORMATION MANAGEMENT

There are vast quantities of digital information stored across the myriad of systems, network devices, databases, and other assets within an organization. Managing the location and transfer of information is essential to protecting the confidentiality, integrity, and availability of the data.

Data loss is the exposure of proprietary, sensitive, or classified information through either data theft or data leakage. Data theft occurs when data is intentionally stolen or exposed, as in cases of espionage or employee disgruntlement. Data leakage is the inadvertent exposure of data, as in the case of a lost or stolen laptop, an employee storing files using an Internet storage application, or an employee saving files on a USB drive to take home.

An effective data loss prevention (DLP) strategy includes data inventory and classification; data metric collection; policy development for data creation, use, storage, transmission, and disposal; and tools to monitor data at rest, in use, and in transit. There are a variety of tools available for DLP. Typical network and security tools such as network analysis software, application firewalls, and intrusion detection and prevention systems can be used to monitor data and its contents as it is transmitted. Specially purposed DLP software also exists with features such as port and endpoint control, disk and file encryption, and database transaction monitoring. These tools may be specialized network traffic monitors or software agents installed on desktops, laptops, and servers. DLP tools have built-in detection and mitigation measures such as alerting via email, logging activities, and blocking transmissions.

The implementation and effective use of DLP technologies can assist organizations in automating the implementation, assessment, and continuous monitoring of several NIST SP 800-53 security controls including AC-4, Information Flow Enforcement; AC-17, Remote Access; CA-3, Information System Connections; CA-7, Continuous Monitoring; CM-7, Least Functionality; SC-9, Transmission Confidentiality; and SI-12, Information Output Handling and Retention.

D.1.9 SOFTWARE ASSURANCE

The NIST Software Assurance Metrics and Tool Evaluation (SAMATE) project defines software assurance as the "planned and systematic set of activities that ensures that software processes and products conform to requirements, standards, and procedures from NASA Software Assurance Guidebook and Standard to help achieve:

- Trustworthiness – No exploitable vulnerabilities exist, either of malicious or unintentional origin

- Predictable Execution – Justifiable confidence that software, when executed, functions as intended."

There are several automation specifications that can assist with continuous monitoring of software assurance, including the emerging Software Assurance Automation Protocol (SwAAP) that is being developed to measure and enumerate software weaknesses and assurance cases. SwAAP uses a variety of automation specifications such as the Common Weakness Enumeration (CWE), which is a dictionary of weaknesses that can lead to exploitable vulnerabilities (i.e., CVEs) and the Common Weakness Scoring System (CWSS) for assigning risk scores to weaknesses. SwAAP also uses the Common Attack Pattern Enumeration & Classification (CAPEC), which is a publicly available catalog of attack patterns with a comprehensive schema and classification taxonomy, to provide descriptions of common methods for exploiting software and the Malware Attribute Enumeration & Characterization (MAEC), which provides a standardized language for encoding and communicating information about malware based upon attributes such as behaviors, artifacts, and attack patterns.

There are a number of software assurance tools and technologies that are now incorporating many of these automation specifications to provide software security throughout the software development life cycle. The implementation and effective use of software assurance technologies can assist organizations in automating the implementation, assessment, and continuous monitoring of several NIST SP 800-53 security controls including CA-7, Continuous Monitoring; SA-4, Acquisitions; SA-8, Security Engineering Principles; SA-11, Developer Security Testing; SA-12, Supply Chain Protection; SA-13, Trustworthiness; SA-14, Critical Information System Components; and SI-13, Predictable Failure Prevention.

D.2 TECHNOLOGIES FOR AGGREGATION AND ANALYSIS

Aggregation and analysis technologies are those that have the capability to collect raw data from one or more security controls or other direct data gathering technologies and correlate, analyze, and represent the raw data in a way that provides a more meaningful perspective on the effectiveness of security control implementation across part or all of an organization than would data from any single technology.

This section discusses common types of aggregation and analysis technologies and their role in supporting an ISCM capability. They include SIEM and management dashboards.

D.2.1 SECURITY INFORMATION AND EVENT MANAGEMENT (SIEM)

To enhance the ability to identify inappropriate or unusual activity, organizations may integrate the analysis of vulnerability scanning information, performance data, network monitoring, and system audit record (log) information through the use of SIEM tools. SIEM tools are a type of centralized logging software that can facilitate aggregation and consolidation of logs from multiple information system components. SIEM tools can also facilitate audit record correlation and analysis. The correlation of audit record information with vulnerability scanning information is important in determining the veracity of the vulnerability scans and correlating attack detection events with scanning results.

SIEM products usually include support for many types of audit record sources, such as operating systems, application servers (e.g., Web servers, email servers), and security software, and may even include support for physical security control devices such as badge readers. An SIEM server analyzes the data from all the different audit record sources, correlates events among the audit record entries, identifies and prioritizes significant events, and can be configured to initiate responses to events.

For each supported audit record source type, SIEM products typically can be configured to provide functionality for categorization of the most important audit record fields (e.g., the value in field 12 of application XYZ's logs signifies the source IP address) which can significantly improve the normalization, analysis, and correlation of audit record data. The SIEM software can also perform event reduction by disregarding those data fields that are not significant to information system security, potentially reducing the SIEM software's network bandwidth and data storage usage.

The implementation and effective use of SIEM technologies can assist organizations in automating the implementation, assessment, and continuous monitoring of several NIST SP 800-53 security controls including AC-5, Separation of Duties; AU-2, Auditable Events; AU-6, Audit Review, Analysis, and Reporting; AU-7, Audit Reduction and Report Generation; CA-2, Security Assessments; CA-7, Continuous Monitoring; IR-5, Incident Monitoring; PE-6, Monitoring Physical Access; RA-3, Risk Assessment; RA-5, Vulnerability Scanning; and SI-4, Information System Monitoring.

D.2.2 MANAGEMENT DASHBOARDS

A security management dashboard (or security information management console) consolidates and communicates information relevant to the organizational security status in near real-time to security management stakeholders. Personnel with responsibility for information security range from a technical system administrator, to the SISO, to the risk executive (function). The security management dashboard presents information in a meaningful and easily understandable format that can be customized to provide information appropriate to those with specific roles and responsibilities within the organization.

To maximize the benefits of management dashboards, it is important to obtain acceptance and support from upper-level management, define useful and quantifiable organization-specific performance metrics that are based on information security policies and procedures, and ensure the availability of meaningful performance data.

The implementation and effective use of management dashboards can assist organizations in automating the implementation, assessment, and continuous monitoring of several NIST SP 800-53 security controls including AC-5, Separation of Duties; CA-6, Security Authorization, CA-7, Continuous Monitoring; PM-6, Information Security Measures of Performance; PM-9, Risk Management Strategy; RA-3, Risk Assessment; and SI-4, Information System Monitoring.

D.3 AUTOMATION AND REFERENCE DATA SOURCES

Managing the security of systems throughout an organization is challenging for several reasons. Most organizations have many systems to patch and configure securely, with numerous pieces of software (operating systems and applications) to be secured on each system. Organizations need to conduct continuous monitoring of the security configuration of each system and be able to determine the security posture of systems and the organization at any given time. Organizations may also need to demonstrate compliance with security requirements expressed in legislation, regulation, and policy. All of these tasks are extremely time-consuming and error-prone because there has been no standardized, automated way of performing them. Another problem for organizations is the lack of interoperability across security tools; for example, the use of proprietary names for vulnerabilities or platforms creates inconsistencies in reports from multiple tools, which can cause delays in security assessment, decision making, and vulnerability remediation. Organizations need standardized, automated approaches to overcoming these challenges.

Automation is an efficient way to enable ISCM within and across domains to capture, correlate, analyze, and report the overall security status of the organization. Automation specifications and standardized formats enable the interoperability and flow of data between these domains. Just about every security tool provides some sort of automated capability as part of its functionality, including importing and exporting data and performing other pre-configured, unassisted operations. Some of these automated capabilities rely on proprietary methods and protocols, while others use standardized specifications and methods. When using a tool that automatically configures devices or changes settings, the new configurations are first tested in a test environment. Some examples of security automation activities include:

- Scanning for vulnerabilities and automatically applying the appropriate patches;
- Automatically enabling security configurations based on a checklist of security settings;
- Scanning for compliance against a pre-configured checklist of security settings; and
- Collecting security metrics from tools and reporting them to a management console in a standardized format.

These are just a few of the many security activities that can be automated. The tools and technologies discussed in this publication leverage a variety of supporting protocols, specifications, and resources to provide the standardization and interoperability necessary to enable ISCM.

The automation specification movement is a community-driven effort to standardize the format and nomenclature for communicating security and IT related information. These data exchange standards create the foundation for automating activities across disparate vendor tool sets, as well as interoperability across domain boundaries. The most mature and widely used set of specifications is the Security Content Automation Protocol (SCAP), which is used to standardize the communication of software flaws and security configurations. This section discusses how SCAP, the National Vulnerability Database (NVD), and security configuration checklists are used to represent and communicate data in a standardized format for performing security automation capabilities and their roles in supporting an ISCM program.

D.3.1 SECURITY CONTENT AUTOMATION PROTOCOL (SCAP)

SCAP is a suite of specifications[50] that standardizes the format and nomenclature by which security software products communicate security flaw and security configuration information. SCAP is a multipurpose protocol that supports automated vulnerability and patch checking,

---

[50] For more information, please refer to NIST DRAFT SP 800-126, as amended, *The Technical Specification for the Security Content Automation Protocol (SCAP) SCAP Version 1.1.*

security control compliance activities, and security measurement. Goals for the development of SCAP include standardizing system security management, promoting interoperability of security products, and fostering the use of standard expressions of security content. SCAP can be used for maintaining the security of organizational systems, such as automatically verifying the installation of patches, checking system security configuration settings, and examining systems for signs of compromise.

What Can Be Automated With SCAP

There are many readily available tools that can be used to automate ISCM activities using SCAP. The SCAP Product Validation Program[51] is designed to test the ability of products to use the features and functionality available through SCAP and its component standards.

The SCAP validation program validates two types of vulnerability and patch scanners: authenticated and unauthenticated. Authenticated vulnerability and patch scanners provide the capability to scan a target system using target system logon privileges, to locate and identify the presence of known vulnerabilities, and evaluate the software patch status to determine the ongoing security status of the system based on an organization's defined patch policy. Unauthenticated vulnerability scanners provide the capability to determine the presence of known vulnerabilities by evaluating the target system over the network without authenticated access. SCAP-enabled vulnerability scanners can be configured to scan connected systems at regular intervals, thus providing a quantitative and repeatable measurement and scoring of software flaws across systems. The use of SCAP-validated vulnerability scanners enables interoperability among vulnerability scanners and reporting tools to provide consistent detection and reporting of these flaws and supports comprehensive remediation capabilities.

While patching and vulnerability monitoring and remediation can often appear an overwhelming task, consistent mitigation of system software vulnerabilities can be achieved through a tested and integrated patching process. A mature patch and vulnerability management program that embraces security automation technologies will help the organization to be more proactive than reactive with regard to maintaining appropriate levels of security for their systems.

Vulnerability assessment and patch management technologies focus primarily on testing for the presence of known vulnerabilities in common operating systems and applications. For custom software and applications and in discovering unknown, unreported or unintentional vulnerabilities in commercial off-the-shelf (COTS) products, vulnerability assessment and analysis may require the use of additional, more specialized techniques and approaches, such as Web-based application scanners, source code reviews, and source code analyzers. These tools, coupled with security control assessment methodologies such as red team exercises and penetration testing, provide additional means for vulnerability identification.

The SCAP Validation Program evaluates the capabilities of configuration scanners that can audit and assess a target system to determine its compliance with a defined secure baseline configuration. Examples of secure baseline configurations include the Federal Desktop Core

---

[51] For more information on the SCAP Validation Program, please refer to http://scap.nist.gov/validation/.

Configuration (FDCC)[52] and profiles created under the United States Government Configuration
Baseline (USGCB)[53] initiative.

How to Implement SCAP

To implement SCAP for ISCM, SCAP-validated[54] tools and SCAP-expressed checklists are used
to automate secure configuration management and produce assessment evidence for many NIST
SP 800-53 security controls. SCAP-expressed checklists can be customized as appropriate to
meet specific organizational requirements. SCAP-expressed checklists can also map individual
system security configuration settings to their corresponding security requirements. For example,
mappings are available between Windows XP secure baseline configurations and the security
controls in NIST SP 800-53. These mappings can help demonstrate that the implemented settings
provide adequate security and adhere to requirements. The mappings are embedded in SCAP-
expressed checklists which allow SCAP-validated tools to generate assessment and compliance
evidence automatically. This can provide a substantial savings in effort and cost of configuration
management. If SCAP-validated tools are not available or are not currently deployed within an
organization, organizations should consider implementing SCAP-expressed checklists for their
secure baseline configurations in order to be well-positioned when SCAP-validated tools become
available and/or are deployed.

To automate continuous monitoring of known software vulnerabilities, SCAP-expressed
checklists and SCAP-validated tools can be used to assess the software assets installed and derive
a mitigation strategy for known vulnerabilities based on risk severity. By performing regularly
scheduled scans of the enterprise architecture with the latest available SCAP-expressed security-
related information, a security officer and/or system administrator can attain on-demand
situational awareness of the security of their networked systems in terms of configuration settings
and mitigation of known software vulnerabilities.

Partially Automated Controls

The implementation, assessment, and monitoring of some security controls may not be automated
by existing tools; however, they may be partially automated using the Open Checklist Interactive
Language (OCIL). OCIL defines a framework for expressing a set of questions to be presented to
a user and corresponding procedures to interpret responses to these questions. OCIL may be used
in conjunction with other SCAP specifications such as eXtensible Configuration Checklist
Description Format (XCCDF) to help handle cases where lower-level checking languages such as
Open Vulnerability and Assessment Language (OVAL) are unable to automate a particular check.
OCIL provides a standardized approach to express and evaluate manual security checks. For
example, a system user may be asked, "Do you have a safe to store documents?" The OCIL
specification provides the ability to define questions, define possible answers to a question from
which the user can choose, define actions to be taken resulting from a user's answer, and
enumerate the result set. One of the benefits of OCIL is that the answers can be returned in a
standardized format, allowing statistical analysis and other calculations to be performed in an
automated manner.

---

[52]   For more information on the FDCC, please refer to http://fdcc.nist.gov.

[53]   For more information on the USGCB, please refer to http://usgcb.nist.gov.

[54]   For more information on SCAP-validated products, please refer to http://nvd.nist.gov/scapproducts.cfm.

D.3.2 REFERENCE DATA SOURCES

NIST provides the two data repositories, the NVD and security configuration checklists, to
support both automated and manual ISCM efforts.

National Vulnerability Database (NVD)

The NVD is the U.S. government repository of standards-based vulnerability management data
represented using the SCAP specifications. This data enables automation of vulnerability
management, security measurement, and compliance. The NVD includes security checklists,
security-related software flaws, misconfigurations, product names, and impact metrics.

The content in the NVD is dynamic; for example, vulnerabilities are updated with new
information such as patch content, checklists are updated, and new checklists are added. As
information becomes available in the NVD, systems are rescanned to reassess risk and mitigate
any new vulnerabilities. To facilitate a standardized distribution of the data, vulnerability content
in the form of XML data feeds is available and updated at two-hour intervals. Organizations can
leverage this standardized data for ISCM automation by configuring scheduled scans of systems
and evaluating changes that may have occurred and any associated security risks from the
changes.

Security Configuration Checklists

The Cyber Security Research and Development Act of 2002[55] tasked NIST to "develop, and
revise as necessary, a checklist setting forth settings and option selections that minimize the
security risks associated with each computer hardware or software system that is, or is likely to
become widely used within the Federal Government." The National Checklist Program (NCP)[56] is
the U.S. government repository of publicly available security checklists. The use of such
checklists within the context of an overarching information security program can markedly
reduce the vulnerability exposure of an organization.

A security configuration checklist, sometimes referred to as a lockdown guide, hardening guide,
or benchmark configuration, is essentially a document that contains instructions or procedures for
configuring an information technology (IT) product to a baseline level of security. Checklists can
be developed not only by IT vendors, but also by consortia, academia, and industry, federal
agencies and other governmental organizations, and others in the public and private sectors.

The NCP provides checklists both in prose format and in SCAP-expressed format. The SCAP-
expressed checklists allow SCAP-validated tools to process the checklists and scan systems
automatically. A subset of checklists also provides embedded Common Configuration
Enumerations (CCEs) mapped to the NIST SP 800-53 security controls that allow for checklist
results to be returned in the context of NIST SP 800-53 control requirements. A checklist might
include any of the following:

- Configuration files that automatically set various security settings (e.g., executables, security
  templates that modify settings, scripts);

---

[55] The Cyber Security Research and Development Act of 2002 is available at
http://csrc.nist.gov/drivers/documents/HR3394-final.pdf.

[56] For more information on the NCP, see http://web.nvd.nist.gov/view/ncp/repository.

- Documentation (e.g., text file) that guides the checklist user to manually configure software;

- Documents that explain the recommended methods to securely install and configure a device; and

- Policy documents that set forth guidelines for such activities as auditing, authentication security (e.g., passwords), and perimeter security.

Not all instructions in a security configuration checklist are for security settings. Checklists can also include administrative practices for an IT product that go hand in hand with improvements to the product's security. Often, successful attacks on systems are the direct result of poor administrative practices such as not changing default passwords or failure to apply new patches.

A checklist comparison can also be performed as part of auditing and continuous monitoring of deployed systems' security, to ensure that the baseline configurations are maintained. It is not normally sufficient to configure a computer once and assume that the settings will be maintained; settings may change as software is installed, upgraded, and patched, or as computers are connected and disconnected from domains. Users might also alter security settings, such as in the case of a user who feels that a locking screen saver is inconvenient and hence turns the feature off.

D.4 REFERENCE MODEL

Organizations can use the technologies, specifications, and reference data sources discussed in Appendix D in an integrated manner to architect an ISCM technical implementation that maximizes the use of security-related information and promotes consistency in the planning and implementation of ISCM. Where possible, this ISCM technical implementation automates the collection, aggregation and analysis, and reporting and presentation of data that is necessary to support organization-defined metrics.

However, organizations face significant challenges in integrating these technologies to enable ISCM. Organizations typically use a diverse set of security products from multiple vendors. Thus it is necessary to extract security-related information (ideally in the form of raw system state data) from these tools and to normalize that data so that it is comparable (at tier 3 level and at tiers 2 and 1). A tier 3 capability is created to enable querying and reporting on the data aggregated from multiple tools covering multiple ISCM security automation domains. Since there are often many local tier 3 repositories covering different parts of a large enterprise, the tier 3 ISCM repositories regularly report data to tier 2 repositories, likely following a hierarchical architecture. The tier 2 repositories in turn report data to tier 1 repositories that may report data to even higher level users. As this data is passed up the ISCM hierarchy, it is abstracted since it is not usually possible or advisable to replicate all low level security-related information at all tiers in the hierarchy. Higher tier users query the lower level tiers to retrieve data. One challenge is the need for a technical mechanism to allow a higher tier query to be passed to lower tier ISCM instances for fulfillment. Another challenge is that in conducting query fulfillment, the lower tier ISCM instances may need to perform analysis of raw data to generate the results. These results may be findings (comparison of raw data against policy) or scores (numerical evaluation of a set of findings) and so a mechanism in the query by which to convey the desired analysis that is to be performed is needed. Ideally, if the requested data is not available at tier 3, then the tier 3 ISCM instance tasks its diverse security tools to collect the requested data.

These challenges can be met through the use of a reference model that describes the types of tools needed, their relationships, and their required roles in fulfilling ISCM functionality. The model either leverages or provides interface specifications that enable integration of these tools in order for an organization to compose an ISCM technical implementation. The model also provides specifications for each tool type so that the tools perform their roles appropriately in implementing organization wide ISCM.

One example of an ISCM reference model that promotes this consistent integration is the CAESARS Framework Extension, described in NIST Interagency Report (NISTIR) 7756, *CAESARS Framework Extension: An Enterprise Continuous Monitoring Technical Reference Architecture (Draft)*. NISTIR 7756 provides a foundation for a continuous monitoring reference model that aims to enable organizations to aggregate collected data from across a diverse set of security tools, analyze that data, perform scoring, enable user queries, and provide overall situational awareness.

The model is based on a set of high level workflow that describe necessary data movement within an ISCM technical implementation. These workflow are realized through the model's subsystem specifications (i.e., requirements for types of tools) and interface specifications for tool communication. One ability to leverage the model is dependent in part on the available infrastructure and the maturity of the organization's measurement program.[57] The functional capabilities of an architecture implemented to support ISCM include data collection, storage, querying, analysis, retrieval, propagation to higher tiers, and presentation.

In the model, data is collected (for predefined metrics or in response to a user query) to include those related to security control implementation and effectiveness. The types of data sources include people, processes, technologies, and the computing environment, (including security control assessment results). A variety of methods, both automated and manual, can be used to collect data. Organizations consider utilizing standards-based methods within tools for performing data collection to reduce integration costs, to enable interoperability of diverse tools and technologies, and to enable data to be collected once and reused many times. Data generated by humans can be collected using mechanisms that use automation and that leverage standardized methods. Collection methodologies are standardized and automated where possible to enable intra- and inter-tier information exchange, correlation and analysis.

Collected data is tagged with metadata when stored in ways that maximize reuse of collected data. Data is normalized for purposes of aggregation, correlation, and consistent use in metrics. Care is taken to store data that has been normalized or otherwise processed with its relevant attributes so as to minimize the possibility of contamination of one metric by cleansing algorithms used in support of another.

The model enables an ISCM infrastructure that has retrieval, analysis, and presentation capabilities sufficient to support reporting and risk-based decision making at all tiers. Metrics are calculated in accordance with the ISCM strategy and the established program. All security-related information is presented to those with ISCM roles and responsibilities as well as other stakeholders including consumers of monitoring information who use it to control operations within organizational risk tolerances in accordance with ISCM strategy (e.g., individuals

---

[57] See NIST SP 800-55, as amended, for more information on measurement programs.

responsible for patch management, security control assessment, security awareness and training).
Data presentation is flexible enough to satisfy diverse data display needs across all tiers.

Figure D-2 provides a high-level view of an ISCM implementation that depicts a sample flow of
security-related information from source data collection, through aggregation and analysis, to
reporting of data to users at all tiers. The ISCM data needs of users vary by tier. For example,
system administrators at Tier 3 may be interested in technical details to support system-level
actions (e.g. configuration changes), whereas management officials at Tier 1 may be more
interested in aggregated data to enable organization-wide decision making (e.g. changes in
security policies, an increase in resources for security awareness programs, or modifications to
the security architecture). Careful design of ISCM capabilities provides each user with the data
content in the *format* they need and with the *frequency* of data collection they require to make
effective decisions. More detailed information on ISCM reference models is available in NIST
Interagency Report 7756.

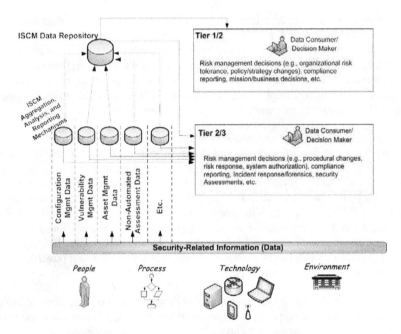

Figure D-2. Sample ISCM Implementation

www.ingramcontent.com/pod-product-compliance
Lightning Source LLC
Chambersburg PA
CBHW060457060326

40689CB00020B/4562